The Rifleman's Wife

The Rifleman's Wife

The experiences of an officer's wife and
chronicles of the old 95th during
the Napoleonic Wars

Mrs. Fitz Maurice

LEONAUR

The Rifleman's Wife,
The experiences of an officer's wife and
chronicles of the old 95th
during the Napoleonic Wars
by Mrs. Fitz Maurice

First published under the titles
Recollections of a Rifleman's Wife, at Home and Abroad

Leonaur is an imprint
of Oakpast Ltd

ISBN: 978-0-85706-204-8 (hardcover)
ISBN: 978-0-85706-203-1 (softcover)

http://www.leonaur.com

Contents

Preface	9
A Chapter on Ireland	11
A Summer in Devonshire	27
A Journey Through France	35
November on the Mediterranean	55
Sardinia	61
Malta	68
Graham's Island	91
Gibraltar.—Voyage Home	97
A Chapter of Less Peaceful "Recollections"	101

Away! nor let me loiter in my song,
For we have many a mountain path to tread,
And many a varied shore to sail along.
Childe Harold's Pilgrimage

DEDICATED TO
THE LADY ELIZABETH SPENCER STANHOPE,
BY ONE WHO
FEELS THE ADVANTAGE OF BEING PERMITTED TO PREFIX
SO WIDELY ESTEEMED A NAME
TO HER LITTLE BOOK.

Preface

To make a long Preface to a little book would, indeed, be ridiculous. I shall, therefore, merely offer the hackneyed, though not less true, assertion, that these *Recollections* were not intended for publication, but have been put together from letters written at the time, and from memory, at the kind wish of some friends; and if they contain anything new, from having visited such places as Bandol and Sardinia, and been within the influence of Graham's Island, it is altogether owing to "travelling accident."

For having *ventured* on the subject of the last chapter, I would hope my title-page may plead my excuse, the *Rifleman's Wife* wishing to preserve, though very imperfectly, a few of those details of personal adventure, during one part of an arduous campaign, which have interested many in the recital.

In conclusion, I would add, that, to the best of my belief, these trifling sketches have at least the recommendation of truth; and where I have borrowed the words of others, it is from finding them so much better than my own, that I think those who take the trouble of reading will agree with me that, in this case, *the end justifies the means.*

F. M. Fitz Maurice.

Cheltenham, Feb. 18, 1851.

CHAPTER 1

A Chapter on Ireland

Erin, the tear and the smile in thine eyes
Blend like the rainbow that hangs in the skies!
Shining through sorrow's stream.
Saddening through pleasure's beam.
Thy suns with doubtful gleam
Weep while they rise.—Irish Melodies.

It was on a clear cold evenings in the month of February, 1827, that we embarked in the *Dolphin* mail-packet from Liverpool, to join the depôt of the 2nd Battalion Rifle Brigade, then quartered at Clare Castle. The sail down the Mersey was sufficiently lively and amusing. Besides the tall shipping from every part of the world which lined its banks, steamer after steamer came boiling past us, speeding on to the busy city we had left, and which was fast disappearing to our view; and, as we stood on the deck in the bright moonlight, and quoted (not for the first time)

As slow our ship her foamy track
Against the wave was cleaving, &c.,

I began to congratulate myself on being an excellent sailor. But, alas for the fallacy of all human hopes! the first indescribable sensation of seasickness sent me down into the cabin, not to poetize, but to remain in "durance vile" till the following morning, when we dropped anchor in the harbour of Kingstown. Short as is the actual distance between the two shores, a stranger to Ireland must be struck by the difference between the light-hearted "ragged rascals" who act as porters on his landing, and their well-fed surly brethren on the other side the Channel; it is as much as between John Bull and the volatile

11

Frenchman, whom (*par parenthèse*) the Irish much more nearly resemble. They drew our heavy carriage and carried six great trunks about three-quarters of a mile up to the inn for 4s. 6d., and gave us all their wit and their welcomes into the bargain.

One merry-looking Hercules shouldered a trunk much too large to go on any carriage, and was complimented by his fellows on having "a gay load that. Bill!" There was no grumbling for more when we paid them their moderate fare, and away they all raced back to the beach to be ready for the next comers. After a plentiful breakfast of buttered eggs, we procured a pair of rope-tackled horses (again reminding one of France) and drove through a pretty country, full of gentlemen's houses, and green even at this season with the bright foliage of the arbutus, ilex, and holly, to Laughlinstown, the residence of the late Judge Day. He was at this time upwards of eighty, but, with a frame as erect, a mind as vigorous, and a heart as warm as many a younger man, presented a fine specimen of the Irish country gentleman and man of the world. Under his hospitable roof we spent a very agreeable week, and made a little expedition into the neighbouring county of Wicklow. Time did not allow of our seeing

The vale in whose bosom the bright waters meet;

but we drove through the Dargle, a beautiful glen, belonging to the Powerscourt family, and though it was a bitter cold day, with the sleet blowing in our faces, I have seldom admired anything more than that wild scenery. At the bottom of a deep glen rushed a mountain stream, sometimes roaring and tumbling over broken fragments of rock, and then gliding quietly on over a bed of moss. The ravine on each side is covered with trees, masses of ivy, and wild plants, broken only by large grey rocks, some of which completely overhung the stream. From the road, which was made for the accommodation of George IV. on his visit to Ireland, walks leading to seats and moss-houses, commanding the most beautiful peeps through the trees, are cut in every direction, and so admirably has art improved on the natural beauty of the place by varying the prospects, that it gives the idea of being of much greater extent than it really is.

Our next object was Powerscourt, from the drawing- room window of which the king is said to have told its noble owner he wished he could change situations with him;—and royalty itself could not command a finer view than those windows possess, and which is terminated by the high peak of the Sugar-loaf Mountain, the intermediate hills seeming to slope gradually down into the ground. We walked on the fine terrace in front of the castle, and through a pretty little churchyard that opens from it; and then, resuming our carriage, drove through the finely wooded park to one of the gates, directly opposite to which is Tennihinch, the gift of his grateful countrymen to Henry Grattan. The sun at that moment breaking out through the clouds, we stopped on a little bridge, from which you have a view of the house, to admire the peaceful retreat embosomed in trees, where the statesman used to retire from the stormy debates of political life, to enjoy, in the bosom of his family, domestic happiness, and the indulgence of the best feelings of the human heart.

Leaving the Sugar-loaf Mountain to the right, the next spot of peculiar beauty (where all was beautiful) that we came to was the glen of the Downs, through which the road runs to the village of Dalgenny, distinguished for its cleanliness and comfort. It is the property of Mr. David Latouche, and is a proof (if proof were wanting) of the good to be done by a resident possessor. Mrs. Latouche (whose exquisite little cottage, at the foot of one of the hills, we passed on our way through the thickly-wooded glen) has established a school in the village, and the houses are of a very superior class to those too generally seen in Ireland.

We drove through the grounds of Belle Vue, Mr. Latouche's place, which is close to Dalgenny; went into the gardens, where the evergreens are considered the finest in the country, and the well-planned hot-houses extend about a quarter of a mile from the house, and returning by Kilruddery (Lord Meath's) reached Laughlinstown to dinner.

Another morning we walked to the hill of Killiney, which commands a most beautiful and extensive view of the counties of Dublin and Wicklow on the one side, and on the other of the Irish Sea. At the foot of the hill are the ruins of a curious old Danish town, and at a little distance is Dublin and its bay; beyond which the eye is carried on to the hill and harbour of Howth, Ireland's Eye, and Dunleary Point, and it is crowned by a building erected by a Mr. Malpas, in a year of great scarcity, to give employment to the poor people,—though in itself not of much more use probably than the roads they have lately been employed on for the same purpose.

In the small but beautiful valley of Glen Druid, which we next visited, is the largest druidical altar existing in Ireland. An immense stone, about eight feet in length, by six or seven in width, and twenty-four feet thick, is placed upon four upright ones, two of which are higher than the others, so that the table is in a slanting position. A rudely-cut groove runs down the stone; it is supposed to carry off the blood of the victim, and I remembered seeing one exactly similar in an altar brought from Old Mexico. The Druids generally chose the most retired places for their horrid rites.

We now stood in the lowest part of the deep little ravine; and when I thought how the stillness of that sequestered valley, *now* only broken by the murmur of the stream over its pebbly bed, had been polluted by human sacrifices, I thanked God that we live in a time when men know that the pure offering of a troubled . spirit and a contrite heart is alone acceptable in his sight, and when the land is no longer "defiled with blood." Under this remarkable stone is a cavity in which, till very lately, a family had existed for many generations. The valley belongs to Mr. Barrington, and terminates in as wild a spot as can well be seen. The stream here falls over some steep rocks, and foams into a little abyss below. Ragged firs and tall pines crown the top of the rocks, and an abundance of wild plants grow down the sides. The path we walked on seemed to hang on the edge of the hill, and on the other side the torrent was a peasant's cabin, perched on the only spot unoccupied by rock or water in a situation much more picturesque than comfortable, I should think.

The following Monday was fixed for our leaving Laughlinstown, and it was with great regret we parted from our kind and venerable host, whom we were never to see again in this world, though his green old age was prolonged beyond the ordinary term of human life, a blessing to all around him. We slept the first night in Dublin, and early next morning recommenced our journey through a flat uninteresting country. We crossed the magnificent Curragh of Kildare—(the town has been in a ruinous state ever since the fire of 1600, which nearly destroyed it;) then passed through Naas, which, from being a fortified place, and the seat of Parliament, is now a dirty little town. The residence of the kings of Leinster was once hoe, and many castles were in the neighbourhood; outside the town are still the remains of a large palace, belonging to the Earl of Strafford, when he was governor in Ireland. We slept that night at Maryborough,—though at the principal inn our rooms wanted much to make them comfortable; but our hostess seemed to think that her repeated assurance that "Lord and Lady Dunraven and my Lord Bishop of Limerick" had occupied them the night before, *ought* to satisfy us.

During our drive the following day we saw several of those remarkable towers about the construction and use of which O'Brien, Petrie, and other antiquarians, have been so divided in their opinions. It is needless for me to describe what is so well known, and which I should be inclined to think were of Milesian origin. Strong traces of their Eastern descent are to be found to this day among the lower orders, who are always the last to retain national peculiarities. Take, for instance, the salutations of the inhabitants of some of the wildest mountain districts. "The top of the morning to your honour;" "*Cead mille falthe roath*;" "A hundred thousand welcomes to you;" "May the world flow upon you, *acushla*," &c.

I remember a butcher's wife telling me once that "Sure himself (by which an Irish woman always means her husband or favourite brother) "had not slept a wink for thinking of that leg of mutton your honour ought to have had;" and the same "*himself*" bringing in a piece of beef, and "wishing it were diamonds for my sake." What could be more oriental? With the exception of the scenery about Castle Connell, where we first came upon the Shannon, and where are the ruins of a beautiful castle, built on a mass of solid rocks, and now partially covered with the giant ivy, which grows so luxuriantly in Ireland, the country through which we travelled presented nothing of much interest till we reached Limerick.

This city, considered the third in importance in the kingdom, was strongly fortified in ancient times. In 1692 it surrendered to the forces of William, and in the reign of George III. was entirely dismantled. Linen, woollen, and paper manufactories are carried on here. The population is dense, and, as we drove through the long, dark, and narrow streets of the old town, swarming with myriads of creatures, whose misery was increased by the cold of winter and the typhus fever, then raging amongst them, I thought I had seldom seen a more wretched place; and I was glad when we crossed Tomond-bridge, and were fairly on our road to Clare Castle.

On the left bank of the Shannon, and in a most commanding position, stand the lofty ruins of Corrig O'Gunnel, once the property of the princely O'Briens. Bunratty Castle must also have been a fine place, as well as many others we passed through; and it is sad to look upon all these landmarks of Ireland's former wealth and prosperity, and contrast with them her present state of poverty and degradation. Even since these notes were written she has been passing through the seven-fold heated furnace of affliction—famine and fever have

15

done their worst, and the evil passions of an excitable race have been worked upon by an artful priesthood to their own undoing. Truly, as her bard has written,

We have fallen upon gloomy days.

May his visions of hope be as fully realized, and

Erin's gay jubilee shine out yet.

As we approached the county Clare trees became more scarce, and when we crossed the ridge of hills from which we had the first view of our future residence there was not one to be seen. The barracks are built within the wails of an old castle, on an island formed by the River Feigus, and externally were promising enough. I had been warned that I should see nothing but bare walls, but still had a lurking hope that I should find a *few*, though probably very common, articles of furniture; but when I saw that only one small square table and two wooden chairs were to be all our allowance, I began to think it rather a bad lookout.

And here I would advise any tyro in barrack life to provide himself at once with the necessary furniture for one bedroom and sitting-room at least: we felt the inconvenience and expense of not having done so, for the assizes being about to be held at Ennisy at which the "great agitator" himself was to be present, it was only with much difficulty, and by paying the most exorbitant prices, we obtained a few very secondary articles. The weather was bitterly cold, and often enough did I wish Count Romford had been quartered in Clare Castle; the chimneys are so constructed that the smoke only rises to return with compound interest, leaving you no alternative but to shiver without a fire, or to be blinded in clouds of turf smoke.

We occupied the third story of one of the houses: "the view," they said, "was better" than in the rooms below; but it was only a view of more extended dreariness, formed by hills which seemed a barrier between us and the habitable world. To the back was the dirty town of Ennis, with the ruins of Quin Abbey; to the right, and all around, fields divided by stone hedges, larger grey stones standing in the place of trees, and reminding one of that valley in the *Arabian Nights'* Entertainments, where the inhabitants were turned into blocks of black or grey marble.

Besides the routine of military duty, and the necessary attendance under arms during the assizes, the officers amused themselves with their guns during the time we were in Clare. Snipe, woodcock, and wild ducks are plentiful along the banks of the Fergus and on the bogs. The only variety the ladies had, with the exception of a ball at Ennis (where the staircase was carpeted with *sawdust*), consisted in a melancholy stroll through the long straggling village (in which a desperate fight once took place between some of the Irish chieftains) to the church at one end, or the Limerick road on the other. But odious as I thought the place, I must do justice not only to the genuine humour, but to the kindly obliging dispositions of the poor inhabitants; of the rich I saw nothing: we were, though not

The world forgetting, by the world forgot,

and I seldom felt more satisfaction than when "the route" arrived for Cashel.

It was on a clear frosty morning in March that I first saw a regimental move. The men assembled in marching order in the barrack-square; the baggage, which always comprises women and children, moved off first. The common Irish car, a sort of platform without any sides, and knocked together in the rudest manner imaginable, is very different to any vehicle we have in England; a raw-boned ragged horse is tackled to this with ropes, and the costume of the man or boy who runs by the side completes the picture. On these cars are packed, one above another, all the chests, boxes, and casks belonging to the regiment; and in every interstice is perched a woman with two or three children, and sometimes an invalid soldier who is unable to walk. These poor creatures sometimes fall off in the course of a long day's march, from cold or weariness; but if a child drops, the car-man, as a matter of course, picks him up and hands him to his mother at the top of a pile of boxes, observing, "Sure, and isn't he a hard little chap that, ma'am?"

Then follow the non-commissioned officers' wives and children, a degree better accommodated, as their cars do not carry baggage; and then the soldiers in companies, with their officers either walking or riding by them, and preceded by the band. I watched them slowly passing under the old archway of the castle, and winding up the hill, through which they defiled. In an hour after we were ourselves in motion, and from that time to this I have never wished to revisit Clare Castle.

We passed the regiment, as they were halting on the road, about half-way to Limerick, and very picturesque the green jackets looked:

some were sitting, others leaning on their arms, all ready to start at the sound of the bugle. While they occupied one side of a rising ground, the 99th, who were to *relieve us* at Clare, came up the other, with a similar train of baggage, &c. It is, perhaps, unfair to compare men who were near the end of a long march to those who were but beginning, but I could not help contrasting the clean, soldier-like appearance and regular movement of the Riflemen, with the soiled uniforms and tarnished ornaments of the straggling parties of Her Majesty's 99th.

After leaving Limerick, we passed over a bleak uninteresting country to Tipperary, rather a pretty town, and one of those that asserts its claim to be the birthplace of Swift. A pair of fresh horses took us about ten (Irish) miles more to Cashel, in the "golden valley," so called from its peculiar fertility. About an hour before reaching it we passed through

Thomastown, a beautiful village belonging to Lord Llandaff: the cottages, all thatched and whitewashed, with green doors and window-shutters, and standing in small gardens, are very superior to what are generally seen by the traveller in Ireland. The castle, a fine pile of Gothic building, stands about half a mile from the road, and is approached through an avenue of noble trees. Our first arrival in Cashel was not the most promising. The people at the inn, who were expecting to fill their house for the approaching Kilkenny assizes, did not like to have their rooms occupied by cheers billeted upon them, and I confess the tone in winch this claim was asserted by some was not conciliatory. After a good deal of demanding and threatening on the part of the gentlemen and vociferation on that of the landlady (a tall, lean woman), we at last obtained rooms; the single officers took the rest, and we had a *salle à manger* in common. A bit of very hard salt beef and a pudding was all the dinner that could be procured for those who were in good humour enough to eat it, while the others amused themselves by attacking the unfortunate waiter every time he came into the room.

After a couple of days spent in this manner, our companions moved into the barracks, which were ready for their reception. As we had to look out for furniture, we remained some days longer at the inn, and I must, in justice to this people, say that, when left to themselves, they did everything in their power to make us comfortable, and apologised for their former incivility, for which there certainly were allowances to be made. They expressed the greatest regret when we left them, and I found here, as in every other place in Ireland, that, if treated with the courtesy one human being ought to show to another, no matter what difference of rank or station, they will do anything in the world for you. "*Gugh ire lagh lath, as gugh iree ilsal lath, as mabernasyht gootragh lath wourneen*," said a poor old woman one day to my husband, for some trifling service he rendered her; which means, "May the day be a lucky one to you, may your adventures at sea be prosperous, and may my blessing always be with you." Short-sighted is the policy which would drive instead of leading; such a people!

The barracks at Cashel are some of the oldest in Ireland, consisting of a low range of buildings on either side, terminated by the commanding officer's house in the centre. But so much more does our comfort depend on *people* than *place*, that, limited and inconvenient as our accommodation was, I shall always look with pleasure to our stay in Cashel; we met there with real kindness, the more valuable because it was freely rendered, without the power of being returned, except in the grateful acknowledgment of memory, that time cannot efface.

We never need leave our own green isle
For sensitive hearts and sunbright eyes,

sang the Anacreon of Ireland; and I never remember to have seen more beauty (with *one* exception, in Italy) than in the neighbourhood of Cashel; and in the very agreeable house of Mr. Mayne, in whose large and happy family circle we spent many pleasant days, the charm of music gave additional attraction. The town is not paved, and the houses are very irregular; but the streets are a good width, and, except on a market-day, when they are filled with droves of pigs (*con rispetto*) and paddies, who are said to trail their long coats after them, and challenge the first person who treads on them, are not disagreeable to walk in. In the modem cathedral the service is performed. The old one, which forms part of the celebrated rock of Cashel, is said to have been the first stone church built in Ireland, some say by St. Patrick; be this as it may, it is unquestionably of great antiquity.

The chapel and hall of audience of Cormac M'Culenan bears date 901. Here, again, is a lofty round tower, built of hewn stone, of exquisite workmanship, fifty-four feet in circumference. The coronation stone of Scone, now in Westminster Abbey, is said to have been brought from the abbey of Cashel. The view from the rock is very extensive and beautiful. On the banks of the stream which runs below, in a rich alluvial meadow, are the lovely rains of Athassil Abbey. Those of Hore Abbey, the ancient palace belonging to the archbishops, lie in another direction; and numerous are the relics of those strong castles of the olden time when, as a country-man once told me, "The *inimy* were hard bye *convenient*."

The archbishop's present palace is a square unpretending brick building; the gardens are extensive, and laid out with much taste; and as we were allowed the privilege of walking in them whenever we chose, I used often to ramble through a path shaded by lilacs and laburnums, that led by a gradual ascent to the ruins above. After a few weeks' residence at Cashel, my husband was ordered on detachment to Fethard, where we took up our abode in an immense mansion, that had formerly belonged to one of the principal families in the country, and was now converted into cavalry barracks. Another detachment was sent on to Mullinahone, and another to Killenaule, for the country was in an unsettled state, and the "Black Army," as they used to call the Rifles, were found to keep them in salutary check.

Mullinahone is a long straggling village, only remarkable for a strong castle, belonging to the family of Despard, which stood a siege of sometime during the rebellion, when all the neighbouring families took refuge in it. We went over it, and saw the loop-holed windows from which they used to fire down on their assailants, and where they maintained their ground till the enemy were brought to terms. The windows of our quarter at Fethard looked directly upon Slieve Naman, or the "Women's Mountain," at the foot of which the whole family of Shea were so barbarously murdered a few years before: it was altogether a locality of much evil report; but whether it was the *prestige* of the "Black Army," or that we followed the simple rule of "doing as we would be done by," I know not, but we passed six weeks perfectly unmolested, going out at all hours, and frequently returning home late at night.

We had the peculiar advantage here of being in the parish of the excellent and talented Henry Woodward, whose beautiful little church, built within the walls of an old monastery, used to be crowded every Sunday by the families from miles round. His eloquence in the pulpit riveted the attention of young and old, of the serious and the most thoughtless, while in his domestic circle he was equally admirable. "*Use hospitality without grudging*" was acted in the spirit as well as the letter by Mr. Woodward, and many pleasant hours we spent under his roof: with a fine voice and an accurate ear for music, he always presided at the family concerts, and the evenings concluded with a chapter from the Bible, with an exposition upon it, followed by an extempore prayer, in which none of his hearers were forgotten. Beloved and respected as this good man was, even by his Roman Catholic neighbours, the plan of his house, which was about a mile from Fethard, was very indicative of the state of Ireland. It was so constructed, that in case of attack, by closing an iron door at the foot of a circular staircase, the inmates could completely shut out the lower part of the house, and be secure in the rooms above.

Among those who showed us kind attention during our stay at Fethard, I must mention the families of Baron Pennefather and Colonel Gough, father to the hero of the Punjaub, whose house was about half-way to Clonmel. We drove there one day, and I thought it one of the best towns I had seen in that part of the country, clean and well built. The 88th, or Connaught Bangers, were exercising in their barrack-square; this regiment, I believe, is essentially Irish, and I never saw a finer looking body of men.

Kiltinan Castle, belonging to a family of the name of Cooke, was another of our drives. It stands proudly on a rock, and was one of the strongholds attacked by Cromwell. The breach made by his cannon is still seen in the wall, immediately below which is a great natural curiosity—a spring of warm water bubbling out of the solid rock.

During the time we were at Fethard, a circular letter was sent to the different officers on detachment, requiring to know, "if their barracks were attacked, what mode of defence they would adopt." The answer of one, for conciseness, was worthy of the "Iron Duke" himself. "I would," he said,, "shut the barrack gates, and write over them 'no thoroughfare.'"

And now, like the *pierre qui roule*, we were again in motion. Birr, or Parson's Town, was to be our next destination, and with much regret we took leave of our kind friends round Slieve Naman, and of our poor neighbours, who surrounded the carriage the morning of our departure with every demonstration of sorrow. I told them we might return. "Och sure, *mavourneen*," exclaimed one woman, "good people never come back to Fethard."

We arrived at Thurles, where we were to sleep, early in the afternoon, and walked down to see the convent. This place has always been one of the strongholds of Popery, and the late synod would appear likely to confirm it. The superior received us in the parlour, beyond which my husband and a friend who was with us were, of course, not permitted to go; but two of the sisters took me over the house and garden, which are both very large and well kept. They tried to make me believe they were very happy; perhaps they were, or perhaps those of the community who are likely to represent things most *en couleur de rose* are chosen to do the honours to strangers. We reached Birr the next day; it is a well-built town, with fine barracks about a mile distant. The surrounding country was once an immense bog, and, though portions of it remain, the greater part has been drained and cultivated, and the roads are excellent.

Ross Castle stands in pretty grounds very near the town. The present noble owner early showed his taste for those mechanical arts which have since led to the perfection of his famous telescope. Having occasion one day to send for a brazier, I gave him a little hand-bell, which had been cracked so as to injure the sound without any mark being visible. He brought it back to me in a day or two, saying that he "and his lordship could not discover the crack." I could not think what the man meant, till he told me "Lord Oxmantown was very clever at such like things," and that he always consulted him in any difficulty.

Leap Castle, a fine place, belonging to the Darby family, is a few miles from Birr, but I did not see it. We used often to visit the cottars in their turf cabins on the bog of Allen, and were always invited to share the "laughing praties" preparing for the family meal. Alas! a sad change has come over these poor people since then, and many a blazing hearth has been quenched. Their generosity, when they had to give, knew no bounds; the earliest potatoes, the most beautiful flowers, fruit, eggs, butter, &c., used constantly to be brought to us; and though our prejudiced little Scotch colonel used to assure me, putting his hand on his sword, if ever a little ragged gossoon ran after us for a penny, that they were "all spies, on my word, all spies," I never discovered any act of treachery among the "native Irish."

One night we were woke by the sound of the bugle, and the cry of "Fire!" but it had originated quite by accident in a row of cottages immediately behind the barracks, and from their all being thatched spread with great rapidity. Almost as rapidly both men and offices turned out, and by their exertions it was extinguished before it spread farther. No "Muggins to the rescue, ho!" could have shown more alacrity than one young recruit on this occasion. He was in at every window and out on every blazing roof, and his example went far in encouraging his comrades.

The open country around Birr was favourable to military manoeuvres, and the 17th Regiment being quartered there at the same time as the Rifles, a field-day and sham fight were given, to witness which people came in cars and carriages from all the country round. I was now so well accustomed to light infantry movements, that I was not so much taken by surprise as I might have been a few months before when the order arrived one day, just as we were sitting down to dinner, that we were to march the next morning to Dublin, *en route* to England! *Many hands make light work.* There were always plenty of willing riflemen to manage the heavy packing; bills we had none; and by ten o'clock the next morning we had turned our backs on Parson's Town.

I never shall forget the weary long drive, with one pair of horses, of twenty-three Irish miles, to Mount Mellick. We passed through Nemo Park, Lord Portarlington's: the oaks and underwood are most beautiful, and I never saw anything like the ferns that grow there; they are perfectly gigantic of their kind, and herds of deer, with their branching antlers, were browsing under the shadow of their fan-shaped leaves. Our children, who were too young to have any eye for the beauties of Nature, were becoming, as the best children will do, very sleepy and cross, and F. M. asked the postboy if it would not be possible to quicken his pace. "Ah, your honour!" said the man, with an inexpressible look of drollery, "and isn't it a *throt* for the town I would be keeping?" At that town we did at last arrive, and, having seen the weary ones in bed, it was no small comfort to sit down by a blazing turf fire to tea; and such an Irish profusion of tea as it was. Besides the common accessories of bread and butter, a *pile* of mutton-chops, and upwards of twenty fresh-laid eggs, sent up like potatoes on a dish,—for two people!

Near Mount Mellick is Cappard. I am not sure whether it is the birth-place of the "immortal duke;" but it belongs to his family, and in early youth he was at school at Portarlington."[1] The notion that brave and soaring spirits are best nurtured in mountain scenery may hold good in this case, for Cappard is on an elevated and commanding situation; while the evergreens by which it is surrounded, and for which it is famous, might be considered as prognostics of the laurel wreath which has since encircled the brow of *the hero of a hundred fights.*

It was late the next day when we reached Dublin. As we were to remain there three weeks, we took lodgings in Nassau-street, and I

1. Since writing the above, I have seen an extract from the parish register of St. Peter's, Dublin, and find that the Duke of Wellington was baptized in that church on the 30th of April, 1769.

had an opportunity of seeing a little more of this beautiful city than on my first visit; but it would be useless to describe what is so well known. I was struck by the width of the streets, and the advantage the public buildings possess over those of London, from the Irish granite of which they are constructed keeping its colour so much better than Portland stone. The view from Carlisle Bridge of the river, the Custom-house, Sackville-street, the Post-office, &c., is very fine. In the Bank, which was formerly the Parliament House, we were shown, among other relics, the ashes of £20,000 of old notes, issued probably at a time when they circulated more rapidly in Dublin than they do at present.

We breakfasted one morning at the Blind Asylum, with a friend who was at that time chaplain to the institution. Like most others of the kind, it is admirably managed. We were shown the system of instructing the poor little creatures, and all their different handiworks,—basket-making, knitting, netting, &c. I remember being struck here, as I had been at Liverpool, by the plainness of the children. So great is the change made in the countenance when these "mirrors of the mind" are closed, that, out of all the number, there were hardly two that could be called good-looking.

Dr. Sandes, the late Bishop of Waterford, took us one day over Trinity College. I suppose there are few more trying examinations for academic honours than what take place in those halls. The bishop himself had some years before undergone them triumphantly; though suffering from illness and a broken leg, he was carried in on a table to the trial.

Another day he kindly took us out to the Botanical Gardens of Glasnevin, a few miles from the town. Among other beautiful plants, or rather shrubs, I remember the finest I ever saw of the coffee-tree in full flower, and of the sugar-cane. The double yellow rose, which often cankers with us, comes to great perfection in Ireland; I never saw anything more beautiful than they were at Lasheen, a place belonging to Sir John Fitzgerald, near Cashel. With the Phoenix Park I was delighted; it has greatly the advantage of our London parks in the nature and variety of the ground, and when the hawthorns are in bloom about the Vice-regal Lodge it must be lovely.

As I before said, I do not pretend to mention, even by name, the various public buildings and fine edifices with which Dublin abounds. The most ancient, I suppose, is St. Patrick's Cathedral, erected in 1190, which contains the tomb of Strongbow, who, with his brother-in-law,

Raymond le Gros, conquered Ireland for Henry the Second. From the accounts that have been handed down, we are led to believe that St. Patrick preached the Gospel in its purity to the pagan Irish. Happy would it have been for their descendants if they could have received, unspoiled by "the traditions of men," that faith of which the mysterious doctrine of the Trinity was illustrated by their subsequently adopted emblem, "Old Erin's native Shamrock."

A few years since, a very tragical event happened in this church. The vaults were opened on some occasion, and a party went down to explore their gloomy horrors. They returned—the trap-door was closed,—and it was some little time after when a young officer, belonging to a regiment on its way to England, was found to be missing. Every inquiry was made in vain, and it was supposed that he must have already embarked. Some weeks after, on the sexton going down into the vault, he found the skeleton of the unfortunate man surrounded by those of numerous rats, from which, by the sword still clasped in his hand, he had vainly endeavoured to defend himself!

Since then, I believe, no one has been allowed to descend.

There is the greatest difference between the whine of a professional beggar in England and the *comico-poetic* strain in which your compassion is excited in Ireland. The boy who sweeps the crossing will hold out his tattered sleeve for a penny, and hope you "may make your bed in glory!" while an old woman at a shop door will be sure to invoke a "blessing on the beautiful lady with the *change!*" or, if this hint be not taken, she will nudge her companion with "Arrah! jewel, and isn't you the lady would be afther giving a penny to?"

I have seen Dublin as it *is*—noble even in its wretchedness—beautiful even with its grass-grown streets. What must it not have been as *was* before the Union, when, I suppose, no capital in Europe possessed a greater concentration of talent; when the eloquence of Grattan and of Hood rang through its forum; when the wit of Curran and the brilliant sallies of Moore sparkled and shone in those *réunions* at the castle, presided over by the most popular of Ireland's Viceroys—the soldier's friend—the late Duke of Richmond! Nor has the *patrius vigor* degenerated in the son. I have heard it from one who had the honour and pleasure of serving with him in the Light Division, that, voluntarily resigning his post on the Duke of Wellington's staff, this young nobleman, then Earl of March, joined his regiment, the gallant 52nd, as captain, went through all the minutiae of drill like a common soldier, and, leading his company into the field at Orthes, there recieved a musket-ball through the body. This was a man who would say to his soldiers, "Come on!" not "Go on!" and what British soldier could refuse to follow such a leader?

Our time in Ireland now *touchait à sa fin.* With regret I left its light-hearted, good-tempered, and kindly inhabitants, and, embarking from one of the beautiful quays which confine the Liffey within its banks, we were soon in full steam for England.

Chapter 2

A Summer in Devonshire

Heavens! what a goodly prospect spreads around,
Of hills, and dales, and woods, and lawns, and spires,
And glittering towns, and gilded streams, till all
The stretching landscape into smoke decays.—Thomson.

A very rough passage of upwards of forty hours brought us into the Bristol Channel. The weather was too foggy to see the Welsh coast, and there were not many on board who could have held up their heads to do it. The celebrated Mr. Owen, of New Lanark, was among the passengers, and, keeping his extraordinary theories to himself, I was told by those who were in the cabin with him that his conversation was most intelligent and agreeable.

Few of our English rivers are more beautiful than the Avon, from the time it leaves Bristol until it debouches into the Channel at the King's Roads. In the stream itself there is nothing to admire: turbid and muddy throughout, it never would be called

A mirror and a bath for beauty's youngest daughter;

but its steep and varied banks so rivet the attention of the passenger that it is but little observed. The stratification of the rocks along the Avon is very curious, being like petrified layers of red sand, perfectly even and regular, like the white streaks in the pebble called the ribbon agate. The crags above are partially covered with underwood, some of them rising to a considerable height, and projecting over the stream. Cook's Folly is always a welcome landmark on nearing the entrance to the river, of which, as of the more distant channel, it commands a beautiful view. It is said to have been built many years ago by the lord of the soil, whose wife, one day, walking in her grounds, refused char-

27

ity to a gipsy-woman who begged of her.

The gipsy then told her she should have a son who should die an untimely death just before he attained his 21st year. Soon after the birth of her son the lady died; the boy grew up healthy and promising, but the father, remembering the woman's prediction, determined to secure him from harm by immuring him during the last year in this tower, which was fitted up with every luxury and comfort to wile away the time of his captivity. The door, after he entered, was closed up, and all he required from without was drawn up to a high window. Mouths passed on, and the year was all but gone; the evening which was to have preceded his emancipation his father and sisters staid longer than usual, talking to him at the foot of the tower of the *fête* which was to have been given next day in honour of his coming of age, and laughing at the gipsy's prediction. Just as they were going, he begged them to send up another faggot, as he felt cold.

The next morning at daybreak the father was at the tower, but there was no answer to the well-known signal. In an agony of suspense he mounted a ladder, and, on reaching the window, saw his son an inanimate corpse before him! A viper, which had been concealed in the last fatal faggot, had stung him in the hand, and the prophecy was fulfilled. The story goes, that the family left the country, and the people, in remembrance of this vain attempt to avert the decrees of fate, named the tower "Cook's Folly."

On the opposite bank of the river the beautiful woods of Leigh Court slope down to the water's edge. Farther up on the same side is the Nightingale Valley, facing the magnificent cliff called St. Vincent's Rock, near which descends the zigzag. The downs of Redland and Clifton are very beautiful from this point, particularly when the hawthorns on the latter are in flower. Turning an elbow in the river, the colossal pillars of the unfinished suspension-bridge come in sight; and Windsor-terrace, long the residence of Hannah More, looks down upon you. You pass the ferry which leads to the park and woods of Bower Ashton, and, in a few minutes more, anchor in the merchant city. As we made no delay there beyond what was necessary to unship the carriage, &c., I only saw, in passing, the fine towers of St. Mary Reddiffe, which was built, tradition says, when the labourers worked for a penny a day, and in which is still preserved a horn of the celebrated cow which supplied them with milk the whole time. This cow would do for a pendent to the dun-cow of Warwick; though, if both tales be true, one was a much more useful animal than the other.

We staid a couple of days at Bath, which I thought was a fine but lifeless city—*point de movement*, as the French say; it might not be the season, but it seemed to me as if "the days," not "of chivalry," but of Nash and Beau Brummel, "were gone, and the glory of" the pump-room "extinguished forever." Only stopping for a few minutes to see the beautiful rains of Glastonbury, we went on to Exeter, attended the morning service in its exquisite cathedral, and then continued our drive over Dartmoor.

The whole of this road is very striking, and Powderham Castle is not the least feature in the very extended landscape. It is quite what Mrs. Hemans calls one of "the stately homes of England."

On reaching Plymouth, which was our destination, we found the transports which conveyed the troops, and which left Dublin before us, had not arrived. They did not come in till late the following day, having been nearly wrecked in a gale off the Scilly Islands. Plymouth from the sea has a much more imposing appearance than on the land side: all the remarkable points, the Breakwater, Mount Edgecumbe, the Hoe, the Dockyard, Drake's Island, &c., are best seen from the water. The rides and drives are delightful, and in hot .weather the advantage of a Devonshire lane, with its thick, high hedges, can be fully appreciated. It has always been a favourite quarter with the military, both from the cheapness and excellence of living, and its various resources in the way of amusement. Boating was a favourite one, and every regiment had its own boat, manned by the officers: that of the Rifles (the Red Rover) used

To walk the water like a thing of life.

Six officers went one day to the Weir Head and back, a distance of about fifty miles, in eight hours. Another day we joined a large picnic party to Cothele House, about eighteen miles up the river; several boats were filled, and each took a share of provisions for the day. Nothing could be pleasanter than the pull up the Tamar. We passed "Thanks," given by Queen Elizabeth to an ancestor of Lord Graves, for some service rendered; passed several other places and some picturesque ruins, and landed at Trematon, to walk through the grounds. Cothele House is placed on a bold knoll on the western bank of the river, in the midst of woods of noble chestnut- trees, whose shade we found very welcome as we climbed the hill. Our dinner was laid out in the great hall, which is hung round with weapons of various kinds, and at one end is a figure in full armour. We were all very hungry, and healths were drank, and champagne-corks flew about over boards where probably once

> *They carved at the meat with gloves of steel.*
> *And they drank the red wine through the helmet barred.*

Dinner over, we explored the house, which is very curious. The furniture is principally of the reign of Elizabeth; some of the rooms are tapestried, and in one was a very singular antique cabinet, some ancient music-books, and drinking vessels. The hall was then cleared for dancing, and the evening was pretty far advanced when we descended to our boats, not without some fear that, beguiled by the beauty of Cothele, we had run the risk of being stuck fast for some hours in the mud, by the going out of the tide; however, fortune favoured us, and, lighted by the moon, we landed at the Government stairs a little after eleven. Many are now gone who were of this gay and lively party, and none more full of life that day than Captain Canning, of the *Alligator*, who to the hereditary talent of his family joined the frank and open manners of the sailor. This young officer died very shortly after at Madeira, of fever, brought on by bathing when heated by violent exercise.

Taking boat immediately below Mount Wyse, we used often in the eve to cross the water to Mount Edgecumbe, and ramble about its forty miles of walks: they are very numerous, but still, I think, must be over-reckoned. However, *they say so*; and I only repeat it, as I do the following story of the late lord, who is said to have been born after his mother was buried. Her body, after her supposed death, was committed to the family mausoleum, and when all the funeral train were gone, the sexton, tempted by the valuable rings in which the lady had been buried, returned to the vault. Great was his terror when, on opening the coffin, the corpse began to move. It may easily be understood that, in his precipitate flight, he left the door open; and it is said that, on coming to herself, the lady rose, and actually walked in her shroud to the house; that she lived many years, and that it was after this her eldest son was born.

The view from Mount Edgecumbe is very extensive and beautiful: on one side you have the famous Breakwater, a terrace built up in the sea—the open ocean and the Eddystone in the distance; on the other, Devonport and Plymouth, the Hamoaze filled, with shipping, the Tamar, and the dockyard. The abrupt rocky cliff to the south is planted with every sort of evergreen and shrub, growing quite down to the water's edge; and whatever we may think of his presumption, we cannot wonder at the taste of the Duke de Medina-Celi, the Spanish admiral, who, during the time that the vaunted Armada, in the form of a crescent, lay-to off our coast, is said to have selected Mount Edgecumbe as *his* future residence in England! May *He "who blew with his wind, and they were scattered,"* ever "preserve our shores from being polluted by a foreign foe."[1]

In the course of this summer Plymouth was honoured by a royal visit. His late Majesty, William IV., then Duke of Clarence, was on a tour round the coast, and it was announced that the duchess was to name a three-decker, the building of which we had watched with much interest. I was delighted with the opportunity of seeing the launch of a first-rate, and it quite answered my expectations. The royal party, attended by the admiral and his lady, the governor and his staff, proceeded to the slip in which lay the noble vessel; a band of music was on board, and her deck covered with people. After some preliminary forms, the duchess, dashing a bottle of wine against the vessel, gave her the name of the *Royal Adelaide*; the band struck up the national anthem; the guns on the battery of Mount Wyse fired a salute, and amidst the cheers of thousands the beautiful ship glided into its future element—*impetus ipse fecit navem.*

A serious accident had nearly occurred at this moment, from the duke's advancing first, as they were removing the dog-shores, or last supports, on which the vessel rested; Lady Northesk saw the danger, and pulled him back. We had gone with some friends in a boat to the opposite side, whence we had a view of the whole; and I never saw a more animated scene. The shore was lined with spectators; the water covered with boats; colours floated at the mast-head of every vessel in Hamoaze, to welcome their royal sister among them; and the glory of an August sun was shining over all. The next day was not so favourable for a review of the troops on the Government Parade. The rain came down, as it does in Devonshire, in good earnest; but his Royal Highness, declining even the shelter of an umbrella, stood it all for some hours, addressing each regiment in turn, and showing a wonderful memory of all the different actions they had at any time been engaged in.

Besides two companies of Engineers and Artillery, the 1st and 2nd

---

1. It ought to be known, to the honour of Plymouth, that at the time of the threatened invasion the town equipped seven ships and a fly-boat to oppose the foe, a greater number than was furnished by any other port except London.

battalions of the Rifle Brigade, the 18th or Royal Irish, the 43rd, and the 29th, were present on this occasion. This last regiment is remarkable for its excellent internal economy, and the management of its schools, &c. There is a peculiarity in their mess, from the officers always sitting down with their swords, since the time the regiment was once attacked in India when they were at table, and were nearly cut to pieces. In addressing the Rifles,—in company with whom, his Royal Highness had served on the Helder,—he went over their history from the formation of the regiment, and wound up by saying, "And what more can I say of you riflemen, than that, wherever there has been fighting you have been employed, and wherever you have been employed you have distinguished yourselves?"

Another royal visitor at Plymouth this year was the Portuguese Prince, Don Miguel. He was as good-looking as a little man with an indifferent countenance could be; was fond of dancing, but had no taste for manly sports, his principal amusement in the morning, it was said, being in shooting cats from the windows of his hotel! A review and some public entertainments were given during the time he was delayed by the badness of the weather. At last, to the great relief of the admiral, Lord Northesk, and the governor, Sir John Cameron, on whom devolved the duty of entertaining the intellectual Prince (as it would have been contrary to etiquette for him to go to the house of any private gentleman), the wind moderated, and he embarked with his suite; but before they got out of the Channel a heavy gale set in from the south-west, and in all the agony of sea-sickness, from which royalty itself is not exempt, he sent orders to the captain "to stop the ship." A lesson from Canute might have made him a wiser man.

The Russian fleet,—or some part of it, I ought to say,—came in after this for a few days. The Russian sailor is a sort of amphibious animal—half soldier, half sailor. The admiral and some remarkably ugly officers came on shore, and some of our officers went out to visit their ships, which appeared to be in a dirty, murdered condition, the sailors, in shakos and boots, lying about half asleep on the decks! In short, they did not leave a good impression, in a place like Plymouth, of the maritime economy of Russia.

A more interesting arrival was that of the *Genoa* from Navarino, with the body of Captain Bathurst on board, who was buried with military honours a few days after; and the solemnity of the scene was increased by the sudden death of a young officer of the 96th, who, when the troops were all drawn up in line to receive the body, staggered forward a few paces and fell lifeless to the ground. It was only the week before that he had told a lady, to whom he was talking in the theatre, that he always had the impression that he should die suddenly. The *Genoa* was one of the ships which had suffered severely at Navarino: being fir-built, every shot told additionally by splintering the wood; teak, from not doing this, it would appear, is much to be preferred for ships of war.

As I am not writing a guide-book, but merely from recollection a few circumstances in which we more or less participated, I have not mentioned one-half of the objects of interest or curiosity in and about Plymouth. The dockyard alone, with all its various operations, from the laying of the keel of a vessel until she is launched, would occupy many days to see, and requires a description I could not give to do it justice. In the fine summer evenings we used often to take a boat and visit the different ships. The *Britannia* at this time was the guard-ship; the *Bellerophon*, now *Captivity*, was the one appointed for the convicts who worked in the dockyard; the *St. Josef*, *Granges*, *Windsor Castle*, and *Ocean*, with many frigates, and every variety of smaller craft, peopled the Hamoaze: there was as much life on the water as on land.

The diving-bell which was used in the construction of the Breakwater, and of the Tara bridge, is preserved near Drake's Island; a lady we know insisted upon going down in it, and of course acquired the euphonious *soubriquet* of "the diving *belle*." The three towns of Plymouth, Devonport, and Stonehouse were at this time separate, the well-known halfpenny bridge connecting the two former; Stonehouse consisted principally of one very long street, chiefly inhabited by—old maids; and one other remarkable person among them always went by the name of "the colonel of the 72nd." I ought not to forget to mention a field, a little distance from Devonport, pointed out as one of the scenes of the early preaching of Wesley; or the small pillar in Plymouth, raised to commemorate the first supply of water which was brought into the town from an adjacent hill by Sir Francis Drake. The streets, all being paved with Devonshire marble, are beautiful after heavy rain, but dangerous to ride in, from being exceedingly slippery.

The market-house at Devonport, though much smaller than the one at Liverpool, is admirably supplied. Mutton from Dartmoor, game from Cornwall, and fish in the greatest abundance, are to be had, from the monster hake to the delicate red mullet and John dory; the pilchard is peculiar to this coast, and there are other kinds I never met with elsewhere. A friend, who came to us from the north, remarked, "that we were rather extravagant if we had such a dish of fish every day;" this dish, consisting of *pipers* and *tubs*, had cost ninepence! Strawberries are so abundant that they used to be carried about the streets in *clothes-baskets* for sale. By a natural association of ideas I must not forget the "clouted cream," which is a *sine quâ non* at every meal, and is more palatable than swab pie, a dish peculiar to Devonshire, composed of apples, mutton, and potatoes.

The winter we spent in Devonshire was so mild, that we had no fire on Christmas-day in our dining-room, and the geraniums and myrtles in the pretty little gardens in the dockyard were never even covered. One serious storm we witnessed, when seventeen vessels were driven ashore under the Hoe, and the whole town the next morning wore a most desolate appearance: skylights were forced in, chimney-pots thrown off, and slates and brick-bats were scattered in all directions. It was now come to the turn of my husband to join the service companies in Malta, and, as we wished to avoid a long sea voyage, we obtained permission to go overland. Leaving our baggage to follow in the Windsor Castle, which was under orders for the Mediterranean, we bade *adieu* to many kind friends and many pleasant scenes, and towards the end of September embarked from Southampton for France.

CHAPTER 3

A Journey Through France

Now let there be the merry sound of music and of dance
Through thy corn-fields green, and sunny views, oh pleasant land of
France.—Ivry.

We left Southampton early on the morning of the 26th of September, with a prospect of "fair gales and prosperous weather;" touched at Portsmouth to take in passengers, and then stood out into the open sea. The sky was beautiful overhead, but it blew very fresh from the southward, and, having spent the day, not as *I would*, but as *I could*, on a sofa in the cabin, the cry about ten o'clock, that "the lights of Hâvre were in sight," was a very welcome sound. I went up on deck with F.M., where different groups were assembling, securing the small portion of luggage that each person was allowed to take on shore for the night. We landed between eleven and twelve o'clock, and we immediately walked off to the Custom-house, a large stone building with strongly-barred windows.

Tired and ill as I was, I could not help being amused at the scene. The long narrow room was full of our fellow-passengers, all on the same errand; some laughing, others waiting patiently till their turn came, and some grumbling at the delay, which certainly very inopportunely kept them from their supper and their beds. These fared the worst, for with an impatient Englishman the French *douanier* has no mercy, but ransacks his well-stuffed carpet-bag *au fond*; we had no cause to complain. The officers, in their green dresses, with the insignia of office round their necks, and who were seated at a little round table, just felt F. M. round the waist, and with a compassionate shrug, and a "*Madame est bien malade*" to me, dismissed us. Our children, who had been playing on deck all day, and had fallen happily asleep, were carried ashore in blankets, and in less than an hour all our weary eyes were closed in the Hôtel de Londres.

I was not well enough the next day to leave my room, but found amusement by watching the different groups of people who came to fetch water from the stone fountain immediately opposite the window. Here I first saw the Normandy *cauchoise*, for all the water being procured from these fountains, they are the general rendezvous of the women, young and old, and, after the little caps and bonnets of our people at home, it strikes one as most peculiar. Steamers were also perpetually arriving or departing from the quay just below; and vendors of fruit, with their *hottes* on their backs, were extolling the praises of their contents; and certainly I never saw anything finer, or tasted anything more delicious, than the Chaumontel pear. They were so large that one was too much to eat at a time.

On Sunday morning we went down to breakfast at the *table d'hôte*, and at twelve o'clock walked to the English chapel, which is merely a large room fitted up with unpainted seats and wooden benches, and was rather a contrast to the last place of public worship I had been in on our way from Devonport to Southampton—the exquisitely finished cathedral of Salisbury.

On a hill which rises behind the town, just beyond the walls, are several pretty houses, principally inhabited by the English residents. I thought the streets very dirty and irregular, but a further acquaintance with the interior of French towns showed me that, by comparison, they were respectable enough. Being overtaken by a heavy shower on our way home, we turned into a café, and got a *côtelette de sauce en papillotte*. Parties at the different tables were playing at dice, and other games of chance, without any apparent recollection of the day. The desecration of the Sabbath is the first thing that strikes a stranger in France. Mass once over, the shops are opened, and the daily business and amusements of life go on as usual. How they can reconcile this to the command, *Remember the Sabbath day to keep it holy* I could never understand, though some of my French friends (and very good people too), to whom I have made the remark, endeavoured to excuse it by saying that the Roman Catholics begin the Sunday on Saturday afternoon, and end it the same hour next day; for which, of course, they give the authority of their church, unsupported by Scripture.

The following morning we embarked in the steamer for Rouen, I shall never forget the first hour occupied in crossing an arm of the sea, which forms part of the harbour; it was dreadfully rough, that short *chopping* sea which is more trying than any other. I was very ill, somewhat frightened, and exceedingly disgusted with the French on board, who laughed, and danced, and sang till they were fairly prostrate; and then it was such a scene! I did not recover it till long after we got into the tranquil waters of the Seine, after passing Honfleur, very prettily situated at the foot of a wooded hill. This place is beginning to supersede Caen as a favourite residence of the English, and now possesses additional interest as one of the scenes in the flight of Louis Philippe and his family. A little higher up, on the opposite bank of the river, is the Château de Tankerville, finely placed near the water, and surrounded by extensive woods.

The banks of the Seine—which is a fine, though muddy river— are rather steep, and covered with wood and pastures; every here and there is a *château*, with gardens in the old French style of high clipped hedges and avenues of trees cut into alcoves, bowers, &c. The numerous orchards were at this time loaded with fruit; and the little villages on the banks, the variety of hill and dale, rock and wood, and the numerous islands beautifully planted, with which the Seine is dotted, would make the sail from Honfleur to Rouen delightful in anything but a French steamer. We met on board some of our fellow-passengers from England; a family party of (as I supposed) a lady with her son and daughter. She had been very ill, and I expressed my hope to the gentleman "that his mother was better;" he looked rather silly, and said, "Oh, that lady is my wife." To have apologized for such an unlucky mistake would only have made it worse, so I took refuge in a safer subject, the beauty of the scenery, and determined not to guess at relationships in future.

The last few miles of the Seine we lost in darkness, as it was near 11 o'clock when we landed at Rouen, and lost no time in finding out the Hôtel de France, *Rue des Carmes*, which had been recommended to us. This is a very large and old hotel, with a square court in the centre. The *table d'hôte* is excellent. The next morning we went to the public gardens of St, Antoine, close to which is the beautiful Gothic church of St. Ouen, formerly belonging to the Benedictines, then to the celebrated Notre Dame of Rouen. The outside is magnificent, but the beauty of the interior is spoilt by the multiplicity of little shrines and images, tallow candles, and faded artificial flowers and tinsel, votive offerings, &c. The great bell of George d'Amboise, and the *grand cheval tout couvert d'acier*, which the verger seemed to think better worth seeing than all the rest, we had not the curiosity to mount the tower to look at.

Our stay in Rouen did not admit of our visiting the library, museum, or other public buildings; we left it the following morning, passing by the bridge of boats carried over the Seine, and near which one of stone is in construction. The river winds so much through the beautiful country we now traversed, that we crossed it six or seven times on our way to Paris. The sides of the road in many places were planted with apple-trees, now in full bearing, and I wondered at their remaining untouched in such an exposed situation, till I heard of the *garde champêtre*, a sort of rural police, who patrol the country for the preservation of the fruit and crops.

It was some little time before I got accustomed to the roughness of the *pavé*, and the noise of the postilions' long thick whips, which is perfectly deafening in a town, or as you rumble through the covered archways of some of the old inns. The horses, both for posting and agriculture, are loaded with a quantity of useless tackle, with a great fleece, tufts, and bells about their necks; the saddle is a heavy, clumsy thing, and "the post-boy his boots and his queue" are just as Biddy Fudge describes them. The towns through which we passed are generally shabby and dirty, the streets very narrow, and lighted at night by lamps winging to ropes fastened to the houses on either side. Before reaching Mantes, where we spent the night, we passed Rancy, a large brick country house, belonging to the Duchess de Berri, in extensive though ill kept-up grounds.

Mantes is rather a pretty town, and I saw the high and beautiful towers of a church at a distance. We had been passing to-day through much of the country ravaged by William of Normandy, when he came over to quell the insurrection of Robert; and here it was that he received his death-blow by the plunging of his horse in the ashes of the burning city;—as striking an instance of retributive justice, as the death of his son Rufus in the very forest which he had depopulated for the gratification of his own favourite amusement.

Our first stage the next morning was Meulan, on a hill, above which is the Château d'Evèquemont, where F. M. had been quartered for two or three months when with the army of occupation in 1815. The family were gone, to whom it belonged, but he had the advantage of an excellent library, which was left in the care of an old servant. We were now really travelling among "the vine-covered hills and gay valleys of France:" not that a vineyard in itself is to be compared to a hop-ground, but, planted as they were here on the sides of the hills, and filled with groups of peasants gathering the fruit, they were very picturesque. As it drew towards evening we used to meet parties returning to their homes: those who had completed their share of the *vendange* would have a wooden crucifix hung with bunches of grapes in front of the little cart which contained the tubs of fruit.

Whenever the carriage stopped, sun-bunt women and merry half-clothed children would come up to offer the finest bunches for sale, and I often wished I could send a basket-full home: to us they had ceased to be a rarity, but grapes possess this advantage over other fruit, that they are so light of digestion that they agree with the most delicate stomach.

I was glad to see one of the richest provinces in France at this season. Apples and walnuts seemed most abundant, as well as grapes; cherry-trees were standing in most of the fields, and the pears were not less large or delicious than those at Havre. Crosses of wood and stone, hung with flowers and branches by the devout traveller, were frequently to be seen by the roadside; and the corners of the streets, in both towns and villages, were always occupied by little shrines containing a wax image of the Virgin and Child. We stopped for an hour at St. Germain's, again recalling a passage in our English history as we walked on the fine old terrace nearly half a league long, which commands a splendid view of the Seine and its many windings: myriads of beautiful little green lizards were glancing about in the sunshine, and some half-dozen *vieux moustaches,* with the *croix* of the *légion d'honneur* to their button-holes, were sauntering along the turf that the feet of royalty and of beauty had so often pressed. The palace, which is an immense high building, surrounded by a deep ditch, rather reminded me of Hampton Court, in its dull grandeur. The inside, we were told, was in a very ruinous state, little being left of what Miss Strickland so graphically describes in her interesting life of Beatrice d'Este, the faithful wife and companion of the fallen monarch who ended his life within those walls.

Once more we changed horses before we reached Paris, which we entered by the Barrière de l'Etoile with a redoubled cracking of whips. A perfectly straight road, nearly two miles long, is terminated by the grand triumphal arch begun by Napoleon, and which workmen were still employed in finishing. On we drove down the Champs Elysées, crossed the Place Louis XV., and entered the Rue Rivoli, where we took up our quarters at the Hotel de Brighton. The interior arrangements of this house were very good, and we had a very nice suite of rooms in the entresol (which I preferred to going higher) for ten *francs* a day, which was extremely moderate.

We ordered our dinner from the "*carte*," where everything, down to *half* a chicken, was marked with the greatest regularity,—a much better plan than in London, where, perhaps, after eating an indifferent mutton chop, you have to pay five shillings. The day was very fine, and we arrived about four o'clock, just "when the world was well aired" and the *beau monde* were all driving about in their carriages. As I looked from the windows into the gardens of the Tuilleries immediately opposite, the variety and gay colours of the ladies' and children's dresses, as they sat in groups or walked under the shade of the fine lime-trees, made them look like beds of flowers.

There cannot be a better situation in Paris than this. You are in the midst of everything, with these charming gardens before you. The palace of the Tuilleries is a much more kingly edifice than any we have in London. On the opposite side of the gardens is the Place Louis XVI., the Place Vendôme, with its beautiful pillar, the Place du Carrousel, with the triumphal arch of Napoleon, once surmounted by the celebrated Corinthian horses. The Rue Rivoli, the Rue de la Paix, the Boulevards, &c, are all worthy of a great metropolis; but in Paris, as in most other places in Prance, there is a want of keeping which strikes those accustomed to the finished neatness of England: from almost all the parts I have named, you turn at once into streets, a parallel to which would only be found in the precincts of St. Giles's. The same inconsistency prevails throughout: in the same building you will see the greatest luxury and the most thorough discomfort;—doors, with latches like those that would be used for stablest opening into rooms hung with satin and decorated with gilding; and while men make the beds and polish the parquets, women sweep the streets and stand at the crossings.

A *chapelle expiatoire* is built on the spot where the Duc de Berri was assassinated; and where the blood of Louis XVI. flowed from the scaffold, a statue is now erected to his memory. These sort of posthumous atonements are characteristic of a people so "given to change." What is "*royale*" one day is "*republicain*" the next, and streets change their names with as much facility as a Frenchman does his dress. It is said that a painter, who was employed by a foreign prince to portray the costumes of the different nations of Europe, represented the Frenchman *alfresco,* with a large piece of cloth under his arm, and, on being asked the meaning of such a conception, replied, that, as "it was quite impossible to catch what was perpetually changing, he had given him the materials to make up as he liked."

We went one morning to the Jardin des Plantes, seeing in the distance, as we drove there, the gloomy towers of Notre Dame, in that nucleus of Paris, l'Isle de France, formed by the branches of the Seine. We spent the day in the gardens, and dined at one of the little *restaurateurs* under the trees. The happy freedom of the animals here (among which is the finest elephant ever brought to Europe), I suppose, first suggested the plan of our Zoological Gardens, as the bazaars and arcades of London had probably their origin from the celebrated Palais Royal. But what delighted me most in Paris was the Louvre: the immense length of the great gallery, viewed from the entrance, is perfectly overcoming. What must it have been when filled with all the treasures of art, whose places are now taken by the French school, for the most part affected in design and gaudy in colouring; but among these I would except a whole suite of the sea-ports of France, by Vernet, which are most accurate in detail and beautiful in execution, and a painting from the story of Paul and Virginia.

The powerful dark figure and deep agony of Paul contrast finely with the delicately-formed and motionless corpse of Virginia, whose feet he is embracing. Her head falls back on the shoulder of the old man, and her white hands are crossed on her bosom in the attitude in which she stood in the vessel when the wave washed her away. Some gems of the old masters still remain. Among several fine heads are those of Raffaelle, and his master, Pietro Perugino; and two pictures by the former one could never forget—one, the portrait of a lady in red velvet; the other, "*La bella Fornarina*" such breathing flesh and exquisite expression I never saw.

A number of young artists were busily employed in copying. The French style, when left to their own composition, except in architectural drawing, is too *maniéré* and *exagéré* ever to be pleasing; but no one could sit for days contemplating the works of Raffaelle and Claude without benefiting by them, and we saw some very promising sketches on many of the easels. The marbles and statues are downstairs. There are several fine heads of the Roman Emperors; but the figures that struck me most were, "Diana returning from the Chase," and "*Il Centauro vinto d'Amore*," both by Italian artists, and both eminently beautiful.

Owing to our short stay in Paris, and the absence of most of F. M.'s friends, who were in the country, I had no opportunity of enjoying

Parisian society; but I saw two or three very good specimens of the old French *noblesse*. The Marquis du Roure, one of the most faithful adherents of Charles X., came to see us on coming up to town for a few hours; and I was also introduced to the charming and elegant Madame de St. Aulaire, afterwards ambassadress in England. The Tuscan ambassador also, the excellent and literary Commendatore Berlinghieri, was an old friend of my husband's, and, had we remained, would have taken us to Versailles; but we were to be in Malta by a certain period, and had still a long journey before us; and that we can little reckon on what is to happen, and therefore it is wise to "take time by the forelock," the sequel of our adventures proved.

On the morning of the 9th of October, therefore, having hired a *calêche* to Lyons, we left Paris, and, though I would gladly have made a longer stay there, I did not quite subscribe to the opinion of a young *attaché,* who said to me, after describing the overturn of a diligence in which he was leaving the capital, "*Nous avons manqué de périr, mais quand on a quitté Paris, madame, on ne désire pas de vivre.*" Taking the road by Charenton and Gros-bois, we passed a large estate, of the same name, belonging to the wife of one of Bonaparte's generals. The park of Gros-bois contains 4,700 acres. The approach to the *château*, which is of brick, is down a straight avenue, formed by a double row of poplar-trees.

The fondness of the French for these least picturesque trees is curious: many of the roads are bordered with them for miles; and I never saw these interminable alleys without thinking of the story in *Veilleés du Château*, where someone is condemned to walk on a plain for thirty years—it could hardly have been less wearisome. The "cric crac" of the postilion's whip used to be quite enlivening on these occasions. We turned off from the road at Brie, to visit a family at the Château de Grégy, in a pretty little park. A servant was waiting to conduct us there; and when we reached the house, we were shown through a suite of rooms, to one where the family were assembled to receive us. It consisted of the count and his lady; her sister, Mademoiselle Louise; her brother, the Comte Etienne, and his only daughter; the old *baronne*, a friend from a neighbouring *château*; and two priests, one of them a young Irishman of the name of Williams, who had been there some years: we were told there were several in that part of the country, and that in general they were greater favourites than their own priests.

I was a perfect stranger to all the party; but so great is the charm of French manners, and so easy and kind was their welcome, that I soon felt quite at home. Our two little girls were pronounced to be *"charmantes, vraiment gentilles,"* and in a little time we were all seated at an excellent *déjeuner à la fourchette* of fish, flesh, and fowl, fruit and eggs, followed by tea and coffee; the former poured out by the count himself, through one of the little silver baskets that used to be hung to the old-fashioned teapots in England. They were all very lively, and, with the exception of the old lady, who was quite deaf, and one of the priests, talked incessantly: they appeared to be a most happy and united family, and I liked their way of addressing each other, *"mon frère," "ma soeur," "mon ami,"* &c.

We are too apt to condemn our more volatile neighbours as insincere, because they are so much more demonstrative than ourselves. I have lived in habits of friendship and intimacy with many French people, and have not only experienced their kindness, but tested their sincerity on many occasions, and I believe they possess quite as much of the latter as we do. I remember one day, when we were living at Nanci, an English lady calling upon me, and saying, "I have just been to B—— (a country house about two miles distant), and the R——s have begged me to dine there today; it is a great *bore,* but they said so much I really could not get off." The next day in came Mrs. R——.

"What do you think," she said, "of that disagreeable Mrs. C——? she knew we were going to have a dinner-party yesterday, and came out on purpose to be asked, and she staid so long, we were obliged to do it in order to get rid of her!!" So much, thought I, for English sincerity in France.

But to return to the Château Grégy. After breakfast the children were taken out to be admired by all the old *bonnes* of the family, and Madame de Q—— took me over her house, of the order and arrangement of which she might well be proud. They wished us much to remain the night, at least; but we had made out our *carte,* and were anxious to get on. The servants were all in the hall, *"pour nous souhaiter le bon voyage,"* and our friends accompanied us to the gates of the park, and stood watching us and waving their handkerchiefs till we were out of sight. We hoped to have reached Montereau that night, but were obliged to stop short at Panfon, a mere posthouse by the side of the road. No tea was to be had here, and I do not suppose they are often called upon to take in travellers.

However, the good woman of the house and her four daughters made up, by their willingness, for many deficiencies. We had soon a blazing wood fire on the hearth, and with milk, potatoes, and cheese, and a chicken, which probably was killed as we drove up to the door, we did very well. Travelling is the best practical lesson for teaching people to accommodate themselves to circumstances; and the sooner it is learnt the better, for those who reckon on home comforts are sure to be mistaken.

We left Panfon at daybreak next morning, and, passing through Montereau,—where, in 1814, a sharp combat took place between the French and the allies,—we reached Villeneuve la Guyard to breakfast. The Seine and the Yonne unite at Montereau, and a bridge is thrown over them. Part of this was broken away during the engagement, and was repaired with wood, but we paid a trifling toll on crossing, which was to go towards rebuilding it.

The next place of any consequence was Sens, which, from the account given in the road-book, I was disappointed with. As we only changed horses, I did not see the interior of the cathedral, which contains the marble mausoleum of Louis XV. and his queen; but the principal street through which we passed was horribly dirty, and the houses old and bad. At each entrance of the town is a heavy and formal gate. Villeneuve le Roi, which we next came to, is a much better place. Here we passed through two very handsome stone gateways, at each end of a wide clean street, and saw the outside of a beautiful Gothic church. The road we travelled over today possessed no peculiar beauty, but the land was well cultivated, and vineyards abounded.

Joigny is rather a pretty place, built in the form an amphitheatre, and with a wide and handsome quay on the Tonne, which we here crossed again. This place is famous for its wine, and for a beautiful *château* above the town, erected by Cardinal Gondi. It was dusk before we reached Auxerre, and we left it too early the next morning to see anything of the place. The roads immediately around it are good, but before we had gone many miles they became very bad, and as it was very wet and cold, and the country extremely uninteresting, our day's journey was tiresome enough. Excepting just about Lucy-le-Bois, where there is some fine wood, and a pretty variety of hill and dale, I never saw a more hideous country than this part of *la belle France:*—tracts of fallow land for miles, without a particle of green or a tree; hardly a poplar to break the dull monotony of the scene. I was very thankful for a couple of hours' respite from cold and jolting, and a good breakfast of mutton chops (though they were seasoned with onions), at Lucy-le-Bois, about twelve o'clock.

The weather continued so bad that we closed the *calêche*, and saw nothing of the beautiful country the book speaks of about Avallon; beyond that, there was certainly nothing to admire, and I do not think we lost much by evening coming on some time before we reached Saulieu.

The next day was Sunday, and, after three long days of incessant travelling, I did indeed feel it a day of rest. It is too small a village to have any place of Protestant worship; but I felt here, as I have done elsewhere in my wanderings, the comfort of that assurance—"Where *two* or *three* are gathered together in *my* name, there am I in the midst of them." There is great abundance of game in this woodland district: we dined on woodcocks and partridges of both kinds: the red-legged is very white meat, but not equal in flavour to the grey. In the afternoon F. M. walked out in the fields with a favourite setter we brought from England. Poor Fan, if she could have said it, would, I daresay, often have wished herself there in this month of October, instead of keeping up with the carriage, or resting, for want of a better place, on the trunks behind.

Very much refreshed by our Sunday's rest, we started the next morning, and our drive was as pleasantly different as possible from that on Saturday. The roads were good, the country beautiful; and we walked up several of the hills to enjoy it more.

At Chissey, a little village where we stopped to change horses, they told us that wild goats, wild boars, and wolves, were to be found in the dark forests which surround the place, and plenty of fish in the streams. I should think it would be *il vero paradiso del cacciatore*.

A very pleasant drive of about twenty miles brought us to Autun. The situation of this town does justice to the taste of those fine old Romans, in whose time it was a considerable station, and some of their almost imperishable works still exist here. The hills of Mont Ju (Mons Jovis), Mont Dm (Mons Druidum), and Mont Cenis, all three covered with fine wood, form a rich background, and the River Arroux winds along the meadows to the left. We entered the town through a gate of the same name—a beautiful specimen of Roman architecture;—it consists of a double arch for carriages, and a smaller one on each side for foot-passengers; above the entablature which surmounts the gate is a kind of gallery, seven arches of which still remain. This gate is of the Corinthian order; the pilasters which divide the arches are fluted, and really appear as freshly chiselled as if they had only been done a few years. The gate of St. André, of the Ionic order, we saw at a little distance on our right.

In the miserable dirty streets through which we drove after entering the beautiful gate of Arroux, I observed in many of the houses and walls, and in some of the pig-styes, large hewn stones, segments of arches, and fragments of pillars, which had once been very differently placed; and a round tower, supposed to have belonged to a temple of Minerva, now forms a part of the Abbey of St. Audrède. This last transformation is nothing uncommon; the celebrated statue of St. Peter at Rome being nothing more or less than Jupiter Tonans: the hand that now holds the keys once wielded the thunderbolt.

The new town of Autun, in which is the inn where we breakfasted, is airy and tolerably clean, and contains one good open square, with a pleasant walk on the Boulevards outside. F. M. once spent a fortnight here with Mons. T——, brother to our friends at the Château Grégy, who was *sous-préfet* of the place, and went to see the famous glass manufactory, of which Captain Manby, so well known by name during the trial of Queen Caroline, was afterwards proprietor. We saw in two or three places remains of the Roman wall which once surrounded the town, and observed, in driving out, a curious pyramidical monument, called "Pierre de Conus." It is about sixty feet high, and formed of unhewn stones, joined together by a kind of whitish cement. It stands in the middle of the field of Urmes, about a quarter of a league east of the town.

The view from the top of the hill, which you ascend on leaving Autun, quite delighted me. The present road is steep, but they are making another, which will make it more gradual. The hills on every side were covered with trees and brushwood, fine grey rocks in many places appearing through them; in the little dells were thatched farm-houses, almost English in their *snugness,* with orchards and vineyards attached to them.

Looking back, we saw the town of Autun, with its fine old gate-ways, and a handsome new building (a school) outside, and, beyond, the three beautifully wooded hills, rich at this time of the year in all the tints of autumnal scenery. For some distance after we left Autun, we traced in different places remains of the famous Roman road. What magnificent notions must that people have had who established such communications between their capital and their colonies! We saw in a field near the road, in one place, an immense stone in an upright position, like the Druidical remains in England and Ireland.

As we left the neighbourhood of Autun, the beauty of the country diminished. About St. Emiland it was one complete vineyard, and as

we approached Chalons it became quite flat. The land is well cultivated and the roads good; and we went the poste from *St. Léger* to
Châlons in a shorter time than we had done any other; could it be
the *prestige* of the name? We drove to the Hôtel du Pare, which looks
upon the Saône, and is considered one of the best hotels in France.
As we remained here a day, in order to take the steamer to Lyons, the
following morning we went to see the Hospital of St. Laurent, on the
other side the river, which is a very fine establishment, and attended
solely by women, Sisters of Charity, who devote themselves entirely
to the care of their suffering fellow-creatures, and really looked most
cheerful and happy in the consciousness of doing good.

Châlons is a large and trading place; the quays extend for some
distance along the river, and the streets and shops are very good. The
country around is a dead flat, and, though it may hardly seem credible,
Mont Blanc may sometimes be seen. The master of the hotel pointed
it out to us from the balcony of our room. This, of course, can only be
in certain states of the atmosphere, so we were fortunate in coming
in for it.

Living, I should think, was cheap in this part of the country, to
judge from the well-supplied market which we walked through, and
our bill at the Hôtel du Pare. We had for dinner an excellent *potage à
la vermicelle,* boiled fish, roast partridges, salad, potatoes, and Gruyère
cheese, with a dessert of grapes, pears, walnuts, and biscuits, and as
much *vin du pays* as we chose, and for this we paid nine *francs,* about
7s. 4d. Compared with a very bad breakfast we had at Bridport, the
day before we left England, and for which we were charged 10s., this
was cheap indeed.

The distance from Châlons to Lyons is twenty-four leagues, and,
in order to reach it before night, we were on board the Châlonnaise
early in the morning. Mâcon was the only place of any importance
at which we stopped for a few minutes to take in passengers; near to
this town is the famous abbey of Cluny. The wine made here is very
good, and it is the birthplace of Lacretelle and Lamartine. The Saône
flows sluggishly on through a rich alluvial country; the banks are flat
and devoid of all interest until you come within a few miles of Lyons, where they are steep and wooded, and would be really beautiful
but for the multiplicity of ugly buildings, grotesque statues, and every
description of tea-garden abomination with which they are crowded:
one would think all the bad taste of Lyons must have exhausted itself
in this direction. It was dark before we were clear of the steamer, and

found ourselves in the Hôtel de Provence, a very large, rambling, and rather comfortless house, on the Place Belle Cour.

Few places suffered more than Lyons during the revolution; there was hardly a point we turned to that had not its tale of blood during that "reign of terror." The cathedral, one of the oldest in France, is of the Saracenic style of architecture; and the church of Ainay is a relic of antiquity. The Hôtel Dieu, Hôtel de Ville, and one of the theatres, are fine buildings. There is a very curious old bridge over the Saône, and the quays on both rivers form a magnificent promenade through the town.

The Place Louis le Grand is handsome; but some of the streets in the old town, into which we looked, were dreadful,—so narrow, and the houses so high, and withal so fearfully dirty, that you could hardly see to the end;—and yet out of these streets come the far-famed satins and brocades of Lyons. Well may it be said that *one half of the world do not know how the other half live.* Little do the wearers of them think of the wretched abodes where they were fabricated. A friend of mine, on putting on a new silk dress, once said to a little niece, just come from India, "Well, Georgy, what do you think of this?"

"Oh! no be proud. Aunt Elisa," replied the infant moralist, "worm made *this,*" touching her dress, "*you* made of mud."

Being told by one of the most loquacious *filles* I ever met with even in France, who waited on us at the hotel, that another *famille Anglaise,* who were in the house, were going to make the same *trajet* as ourselves the next day, from Lyons to Avignon by the Rhône, my husband sent up his card, which was returned by a visit from Col. G——; and, our numbers being nearly equal, it was soon arranged that we should take part of one of the *bâteaux de poste* between us. These boats are very large, but put together in the rudest way imaginable; the force of the current carries them down in a couple of days to Avignon, but as it would take a month to drag them up against it, they are generally broken up for firewood when the voyage is over. Benches go all round them, and the centre is covered with an awning. We were all on the quay from which we were to embark by six o'clock. At one end of the boat were some French country-people, the *conducteur* and his men, and a pair of little Calabrian horses belonging to Col. G——; our luggage occupied the centre; and, at the other end, the carriage and a tolerably comfortable arrangement of seats for ourselves. It was a bright, clear, autumnal morning, and again we saw, looming large in the distance, "the Monarch of Mountains," with "his diadem of snow."

48

The junction of the two rivers is very fine, but it is curious to observe how long they flow on together without appearing to amalgamate— the bright blue Rhône, and the turbid waters of the Saône, each keeping their natural colour, till at last they become as one.

We landed at Tournon, a small place on the right-hand bank of the river, for our mid-day meal, and then taking again to our boat, glided quietly on to Valence, where we were to spend the night. The scenery the whole way was most striking. Comparing it with the Rhine, I should say that one was like a beautiful maiden; the other like a magnificent matron. The banks of the Rhine rise at once from the river; in some places they are considerably steep: those of the Rhône, by receding, afford a much greater extent of landscape; and the castles and ruins, though less frequent in occurrence, are of a grander character— dark and frowning, like the mailed knights who used to issue from their portals.

About eighteen miles after leaving Lyons we came to Vienne, near which is Mont Pilate, from whence, tradition says, Pontius Pilate precipitated himself. Be this as it may, I believe he ended his days at Vienne, which was then a Roman colony of considerable importance. The remains of a theatre, amphitheatre, and several traces of aqueducts, are to be seen here; and in the river are still the piles of an old Roman bridge, which must have led from the town to a fine castle on the opposite side. After leaving Vienne, we passed under the famous Côte Rôtie, so well known for its wine, and of which we drank a bottle in our boat. The river in this part is narrow, and the banks clothed with vineyards; but it opens out again below, and, before reaching Valence, receives into its waters those of the Isère, fresh from the mountains of Savoy.

The sun was setting gloriously behind the western hills, and as the boatmen chanted their vesper hymn, accompanied by the splash of the oars, with which they used occasionally to steady the boat where the current was more strong than usual, I thought I had seldom felt anything more enjoyable. Half our party were asleep when we passed one place, where rocks, rising out of the water which bubbled and foamed over them, rendered the navigation a little difficult; and I remembered it was probably the very spot of which Madame de Sévigné speaks of the "*rochers blancs*" in "*ce diable du Rhône,*" which had so nearly upset the boat of Madame de Grignan on one of her journeys to Provence.

Valence is an old irregular town; its finest ruin is that of the *façade* of a fine Gothic castle. The name, we were told by a French soldier

on board, was given in consequence of a dispute among the first settlers as to the site of their future town, which was to be determined
by throwing a lance: the most skilful of the party hurled his with the
exclamation, "*Va Lance*," and the name remained with the rising city.
I do not know whether hydropathy is in fashion at Valence, but no
patient of Dr. Gully could have desired *wetter sheets* than were given
us that night; and as drying would have been too long a process, and
the inn did not seem to afford any others, we resigned ourselves that
night to do without.

It was with great delight next morning we hailed a bright sunrise,
for we were entering upon classic ground to all admirers of Madame
de Sévigné. Those who have never read them before, should look
over her charming letters before descending the Rhône—passages of
them were perpetually recurring to me. The "*Château Royal de Grignan qui sent bien les anciens Adhémars*" is not within sight of the river;
but we passed by Montelimart, at a little distance from the left bank,
which is so often mentioned, and from whence she dates one of her
letters after leaving Grignan. We passed, also, today another vineyard,
celebrated for its wine (the Côteau de l'Hermitage, near Drôme), and
some beautiful castles and fine bridges.

I sat the greater part of the day on the *barouche*-box of Colonel G.'s
carriage, and felt as if I could never be weary of the magnificent prospect on either side. But the point of greatest interest was to come—
the celebrated Pont Saint Esprit, with its five-and-twenty arches, only
a few of which are navigable, owing to the shifting of the sand after
heavy floods, as well as to the bed of the river being here full of rocks,
and the current there peculiarly rapid. Madame de Sévigné writes to
her daughter, "*Je vous conjure, ma chère enfant, si vous vous embarquez, de
descendre au Pont Saint Esprit;*" and Mrs. G. and I had made the same
stipulation.

Not knowing exactly when we were to expect this dangerous locality, she got into her carriage, and was reposing very quietly with the
blinds down; and I had descended into the boat, where the children
were at play, leaving the gentlemen on the box. Every bridge we came
in sight of, "Is this the *Pont Saint Esprit?*"

"Of course it is," was the answer, till I was fairly thrown off my
guard. At last we came to one, and I thought I saw a look of intelligence pass between my husband and the *conducteur*, but I said nothing,
as it was then too late to attempt to get out. There was a sound as of
water rushing over a rocky bottom; we sat quite still; the boatmen lay-

to on their oars, and in less time than it takes me to write it, we had shot through the arch, and were again gliding quietly on, and looking back on the formidable *Pont Saint Esprit!* We landed afterwards to dine at the little town of Bourg St. André, looked up at the lofty Roque Maure (on a high cliff) on our right hand, and did not reach Avignon till after the moon had been shining some time on

> *The blue rushing of the arrowy Rhône;*

and a better idea of the character of this fine river cannot be given than in what these words convey. I have seen it since, and after seeing much that was beautiful in nature in other places; but it was with undiminished admiration of the grandeur of its scenery.

At Avignon one begins to feel what the *vrai midi* is;—there is a balminess in the air, particularly at night, to which we are unaccustomed in our more northern climes. "*Mais quels orangers,*" writes Madame de Sévigné, "*quels laurier-roses, et de grenadiers! ils ne craignent que d'être trop parfumés: jamais il ne s'est vu un si beau pays ni si délicieux; vous comprenez ses délices par ceux d'Italie.*" We found Madame Pierron's hotel so comfortable that we determined to remain a couple of days, and I was glad to be able to walk about this fine old city, so full of historic interest. The houses, which are all built of stone, have a greater air of comfort about them than is generally seen in France; the streets are tolerably wide, and very quiet.

We walked up the hill, on which are the ruins of the Papal Palace, and from whence there is a fine view of the surrounding country, laid like a map at your feet: we followed from there the course of the mighty Rhône for many miles. There is another fine view of the town, and of the *boulevard* which surrounds it, from a very long bridge thrown across the river. Of course we visited the tomb of Laura, in what was once the church of the Cordeliers, but which is now turned into a garden within the walls: five small cypress-trees surround the stone. It was in the church of St. Clair Petrarch first saw her, and in the same church, at the same hour, twenty-one years afterwards, "*cette lumière s'est e'teinte,*" he writes, "*ce soleil a quitté le monde où il brilloit.*" I never saw more beautiful grapes than those this garden produces. I must again quote from Madame de Sévigné:—"*Les muscats sont comme des grains d'ambre, que l'on peut croquer, et qui vous feraient fort bien tourner la tête, si vous en mangez sans mesure, parceque c'est comme si l'on buvait à petits traits du plus exquis vin de St. Laurent.*"

A lovely evening closed a beautiful day, and we sat out till late in the balcony, *au premier* of the Hôtel de l'Europe, which looks down into a court planted with acacias, and with a fountain in the middle. We parted there from our agreeable fellow-travellers Colonel and Mrs. G., as our roads no longer lay together. They were to start in the morning for Nice, and we to pursue our route to Marseilles. If by any chance this little *recollection* ever comes in their way, they will see that the *agrément* of our voyage down the Rhône in their society has not been forgotten.

We had arranged to diverge a little from our road in order to visit Vaucluse, which we reached about midday,—descending from the carriage at the little inn of "*Les deux Lauras*," (query, Who was the second?) and declining both a dinner under its roof and the company of a guide, we pursued our way up the narrow valley through which the Sorgue, now a little brook, threads its way from the source of those "*chiare fresche dolce acque*," which have been so immortalized. The bed of the stream is covered with a kind of long and beautifully green moss: on one side are the "*verde colle*," of which the poet speaks, now covered with vines and olives; and on the other, rocks rose almost perpendicularly to a considerable height. The fountain itself is in a sort of natural grotto, quite impervious to the rays of the sun, and the water is exquisitely cool and clear.

After emptying our little basket of provisions, and taking a draught of the water, and after our favourite dog (oh, profanation of the shade of Laura!) had enjoyed a plunge "*ove le belle membra posa colei*," we prepared to return by the path on the opposite side of the one by which we had come up.

We were already within sight of some houses belonging to a papermill at the entrance of the valley, and saw a woman from one of the windows beckoning to us to come on, and pointing to the cliff above. In the course of another minute a large block of stone dropped on our path: Mrs. R., with our youngest child in her arms, was a step or two in front—we so near behind, that there was little more than room for it just to fall between us. We hastened on to the house; but the people, alarmed, I suppose, at my husband's determination to bring the whole thing before the *préfet*, would give no further explanation, and pretended the stone had been precipitated by some sheep grazing at the top, where the earth might be loose, &c.

But it was. no "rolling stone" which so nearly put an end to our wanderings; it was evidently thrown by no friendly hand, and we had every reason to suppose it was that of the sinister-looking landlord of "*Les deux Laures*," whose dinner and services we had declined: he was not to be found when we reached the inn; was gone, they said, to a commune at some distance; and as there was little chance of getting any satisfaction, we got into the carriage and pursued our way, with renewed thankfulness to Him whose protecting arm had been so mercifully extended over us in the valley of Vaucluse. Little of beauty, and less of poetry, seems to exist among its inhabitants, who appeared to think the great attraction of the place consisted in the particularly large eels which are caught in the Sorgue, and which, they said, people came from miles round to eat! Nothing more of incident happened this day.

We did not reach Pont Royal, which is only a posthouse by the roadside, till between eleven and twelve, and it was bad hearing that they were quite full. We were so tired that we would have slept in a barn rather than go on, and felt exceedingly obliged to a courier of Lady C—— (who was on her way to the baths of Aix), who gave up his room to us. One thing you are always sure of in France, be the rest of the accommodation ever so indifferent—a good clean bed and plenty of linen; even in the small cabarets we were obliged to put up at, they always gave us table-napkins. We breakfasted the following morning at Aix, famous for its mineral springs, and also as being the first Roman settlement in France. The hotel stands in a very wide handsome street—more, indeed, like a "*place*" than a street; and, if I mistake not, the remains of an old Roman road are to be seen very near. Leaving Aix, we passed through Lambesc, where Monsieur de Grignan used to go, *en qualité de grand seigneur*, to attend the *assemblée des états généraux*. The rest of our drive to Marseilles was nothing remarkable. As we approached the coast the soil became chalky, and the country more barren.

Olive and juniper trees had taken the place of trees of a bright foliage, and I frequently observed the cypress by the roadside, which, perhaps from association, struck me as having a gloomy effect.

We reached Marseilles in tolerable time, and drove, as we had been recommended, to the Hôtel des Empereurs, Rue Cannebières, the master of which had been *chef de cuisine* to one of the Allied Powers, and whose good table proved he had not forgot his art. Marseilles is one of the ancient cities of France, and used to be known as "the Athens of Gaul:" it is still of much importance, both as a sea-port and as a place of great foreign trade. As usual, the old part of it is dirty and wretched, but there are many fine streets, and squares, and public buildings, in the new town; still I did not admire it so much as I had done places of less consideration. It might be, that twice I saw it under circumstances of much local depression—once under the visitation of cholera, and this summer the smallpox had raged in it like plague. Marseilles has suffered greatly from epidemics. The great plague which devastated it in 1720, and the noble self-devotion of Monsieur de Belzunce, "Marseilles' good bishop," will long be remembered. The English consuls family, with whom we dined, gave us a melancholy history of the fatal effects of the smallpox.

Many houses were shut up in consequence, as the families had gone into the country. The villas around the town are extremely numerous, and some of them have beautiful gardens: every one who can afford it has one of these *bastides*, as they are called, for the summer.

The cathedral is a carious Gothic edifice, said to be built on the ruins of a Temple of Diana. The botanical gardens are very extensive, and beautifully laid out. We walked, or rather climbed, one evening, up a hill outside the town, on which is built a chapel, called "*Notre Dame de la Garde.*" It commands a magnificent view, not only of the town of Marseilles and all the surrounding country, but of the busy port below, and the far-stretching waters of the blue Mediterranean, and is peculiarly resorted to by sailors before and after their distant voyages. It was hung with votive offerings of every description, commemorative of deliverance from many perils by sea.

At this time there were no steamers between this port and Malta, and being disappointed in obtaining a passage which we ought to have had in the governor's yacht (then about to return to the island), we freighted a small vessel, which had been used as a packet, and was then lying in the port of Marseilles. The ordinary passage was one of five or six days; we therefore, laid in a stock of the necessary provisions, made a few more purchases from the well-stored shops of Marseilles, and, in happy ignorance of our future fate, embarked in the *Susan*, in the afternoon of the 1st of November. Our first experience of the Mediterranean I shall give in the following chapter.

CHAPTER 4

November on the Mediterranean

And the winds
Burst thro' their bonds of adamant, and lashed
The weltering ocean, that so lately lay
Calm as the slumbers of a cradled child,
To a demoniac's madness.—Alaric Watts.

The harbour of Marseilles might almost be called a small salt-water lake: it runs up into the land for about half a mile, and is a quarter of a mile wide; the entrance does not exceed above a hundred yards, being confined by projecting rocks, on which are built two forts, known as the Château d'If and the Château d'Or. We went on board, expecting to have sailed that day, but it happened to be *Le Toussaint*, a great festival in the Romish church, which our captain thought a sufficient excuse for not weighing anchor till the following morning. The harbour of Marseilles is said to be capable of containing 1,200 vessels, but is not of sufficient depth to float ships of war. From the absence of tide in the Mediterranean, its waters, which receive all the drains, &c., of the town, are exceedingly offensive. Surely such a body of stagnant water, occupying such a central position in it, must greatly contribute to the frequent epidemics which prevail. What with the very bad smell, and the incessant ringing of the bells in all the churches around us, we have no very pleasant recollection of the port of Marseilles.

Early the following morning we cleared it, and had then an opportunity of judging of the accuracy of Vernet's view, which we had so much admired at the Louvre. The wind being against us, we did not make much way, and it was not till evening closed in that we quite lost sight of the elevated chapel of "*Notre Dame de la Garde.*" The two next days it was exceedingly rough, and we made but little progress.

The vice-consuls at Marseilles, who were agents for our vessel, had promised us a British captain and crew; but we found the one had never sailed in that capacity before, and the other were Maltese. By a miserable subterfuge, saying they were *British* subjects, Messrs. Mecklenburgh and Richardson tried to excuse themselves for this breach of faith; and as our time now was fast drawing to a close, we had no alternative but to take them.

The Maltese are notoriously bad sailors; their great word at sea being *appoggiare*, which is tantamount to what we should call "hugging the land." They have little notion of steering by the compass; it is from point to point they take their reckonings, and into these *un*-seaworthy hands we were now committed. It was little wonder, then, that, after beating about at the mercy of the winds for some days, we missed stays in endeavouring to weather a headland off Toulon, and were in the greatest danger. The sea was running mountains high; the captain had lost all command, both of himself and his men, who, instead of listening to orders, were calling upon the Virgin and all the Saints to come to their aid, while they were letting the ship fast drive upon the rocks.

There was no time for ceremony, and my husband, taking his pistols on deck, declared he would shoot the first man who did not instantly obey. This brought them a little to their senses, and, after much difficulty and far more noise from our six Maltese sailors than would have been heard among a hundred English ones in a similar situation, we succeeded in casting anchor in a fine natural bay to the west of Toulon, opposite the little fishing village of Bandol.

As there was every appearance of the storm continuing, and the prosecution of our voyage was therefore impossible, my husband went ashore in the little boat, with the captain and three of the men, to see what accommodation could be found. They might have been away an hour, but it appeared more like a month: it was a dark, cold, cheerless 5th of November;—one man and a boy alone were left on board; and it was only by fixing my eye steadily on some object on shore that I could satisfy myself we were not drifting away into that stormy sea. At last they returned, and we were conveyed to land, glad enough to get there after what we had suffered. The only *cabaret* in the village gloried in the sign of the Lion d'Or, and to this we bent our steps: one room, of very moderate dimensions, was all the accommodation it afforded, and into this we were ushered, with the worst possible grace, by the landlady. She was a perfect Hecate in appearance, and did not belie her looks.

The first thing that raised her indignation was a request for some warm water, for a bath for the children; such a thing had never been heard of, and she went downstairs grumbling and scolding the whole way. The house was built so close upon the sea, that anything we threw down from our window would fall directly into it;—in all but the motion, we were almost as much at sea in it as in the *Susan*. The village consisted of one long dirty street, stretching along the shore, and our daily walk was out at one end or the other. My husband extended his by rambling over the line of hills, which were immediately behind the village; and sometimes, like Robinson Crusoe, he paid a visit to the ship, and brought back any little thing we might require, or some of our books, to help to wile away the time.

The wine and olive are the only vegetation to be seen about Bandol: from the former an excellent red wine is made, little inferior to port, and several Dutch vessels in the bay were busily employed in taking it off. Beyond these hills was a wide range of comparatively barren country, affording only a scanty pasturage for the goats that browsed upon it; of cattle, we saw none. There are few things more uncomfortable than to find yourself reduced to your last shilling in a remote corner of a distant land, and this was our case at Bandol. Never anticipating the necessity for money until we landed in Malta, we had taken no more on board with us than what happened to remain of our last draft. This was nearly exhausted; and how were we to get more where there was no such thing even as a post?

At last F. M. determined on going over to Toulon, and, having hired a horse, set off on a weary ride there and back of more than thirty miles: he came back in the evening tired and silent. After a little time, "Where is the money?" said I, and he held up the empty bag! Toulon not being named in our letter of credit, the bankers had refused to advance a *sous*. However, next morning, a goodnatured little consul lent us twenty dollars, and a butcher having occasion to go over to Marseilles a day or two after on business, we were able to repay him at once by an order on the banker there. I do not know whether it be an established fact in natural history, that sea-sickness is among the ills that fowl as well as "*flesh* is heir to."

With our stock of provisions from Marseilles we had taken four couple of chickens. The poor creatures looked almost as woebegone as ourselves when we landed at Bandol. The old lady of the Lion d'Or had some in her *basse cour*, which were fattening *pour les noces* of one of her daughters. My husband exercised his diplomatic powers in effecting an exchange, and, lest she might retract, it was no sooner a *fait accompli* than he had them all killed, knowing it would be better to eat cold chicken for a week than embark our unhappy poultry again, and we felt no compunction at getting at least a couple of good meals out of this horrid termagant.

On a complaint that was made one day to her husband, who was a quiet sort of man, of some incivility, he shrugged his shoulders, and said, "*Mais, monsieur, que voulez vous? est-ce que vous ne savez pas le proverbe. Provençale brutale?*" We could say no more, for he was surely more to be pitied than we were. It is a curious thing, but one I have often observed, and higher authorities, I believe, have made the same reflection, that often in the most beautiful scenery the human race appears to be the most degraded. We experienced this at another time all down the banks of the Rhône; we found it to be the same in that exquisite country between Gaeta and Itri; we had an instance of it at Vaucluse; and the people of Provence, in general, are a very different race from the time when

> *Gaily the troubadour touched his guitar,*
> *As he was hastening home from the war,*
> *Singing, 'From Palestine hither I come,*
> *Ladye love, ladye love, welcome me home.'*

We had been thirteen days wind-bound at Bandol, when we were woke one night by a loud rapping at the door, and the voice of the captain, calling out, "*Signore! Signore! il vento è favorevole, bisogna partire.*" We had been too long wishing to go, to make long delay; our poor little children were taken up from their beds; our *adieus* were soon made at the Lion d'Or, and we groped our way in the darkness down to the shore, where the little boat was in waiting, and in which we had to go rather more than a mile, between twelve and one o'clock, in the open sea, before we reached the vessel—such a nocturnal expedition, on the 18th of November, as I hope never to repeat.

As our ship, impelled by the favourable gale, was ploughing through the waters, the captain exclaimed, with exultation, "*Cammina la Susan!*" and I went down into the cabin, hoping that two or three days at farthest would "bring us to the haven where we would be." When daylight came we had lost sight of the iron-bound coast of Toulon, but daylight brought with it a disagreeable discovery. We found that while we were on shore the sailors had helped themselves to our provisions, of which they had taken the lion's share! For this aggression on the high seas there was no redress; and really these poor men, who only acted on one of the first principles of nature, "self-preservation," were less to be blamed than those who had sent them out so badly provided.

We had brought a little with us from Bandol, but it would have been as nothing to a starving crew; and I really do not know what we should have done, if most fortunately the next day we had not fallen in with some French vessels returning from taking supplies to the fleet that was at that time off Navarino. Our boat was lowered, and my husband and the captain went alongside their convoy, which was a ship-of-war, and told them our situation. They immediately gave a supply of beef, biscuit, &c., taking a receipt for the same, and an order on the underwriters of the *Susan*, who were obliged to defray the expense; and when they heard there were children on board, they kindly ordered a basket of dates as a present.

The weather, which had so far been favourable, now changed. I never shall forget the angry look of the sky that evening, before I went below for the night. The sun was setting in a bank of clouds, heavy masses were gathering all around, and the wind was blowing in those short fitful gusts which generally presage a storm, and before morning it blew a heavy gale from the south-east. For three days and nights I never left my mattress, which was stretched on the floor of the cabin; but even *there* was something to be learnt—I ascertained, *in propriâ persona,* that salt-water does not give cold.

Many times, in those three terrible days of storm and tempest, we were perfectly drenched, without the power of changing to dry things, and yet no one was the worse for it afterwards; and never did I so fully appreciate the beauty of the 107th Psalm, or feel the truth, that it is *those who go down into the sea in ships, and occupy their business in deep waters—these men see the works of the Lord, and his wonders in the deep; for at His word the stormy wind ariseth, which lifteth up the waves thereof.*

I remember one moment of dreadful agony, in which, as someone has said, "*one seemed to live a thousand years.*" Our children had been carried on deck for a little fresh air (for the hatchways were obliged to be down), and, with Mrs. R., were fastened on to one of the hencoops. Their father had left them for a minute to see if I wanted anything, when the vessel gave a tremendous lurch, which was followed by a dreadful scream. Of course, we thought nothing less than that all were carried overboard. He rushed to the foot of the companion-ladder as fast as the boxes of tin which filled the main cabin would allow; and the inexpressible relief of hearing that it was only a favourite doll which had found a watery grave I cannot describe.

The vessel in which we were, and which had been built for a packet between Marseilles and Malta, had been confiscated for smuggling tobacco, and, as we afterwards found out, had remained long enough in the foul waters of the former port to get quite unfit for sailing, from the dirty state she was in. As it seemed impossible to proceed, we were obliged again to "*appoggiare*," and Sardinia being the nearest land, it was resolved to make for it. Our jibboom had been carried away, and our sails were so split, that we were almost under bare poles. In this state, happy were we when, about midday of the 24th, we cleared the bar at the entrance of the harbour of Cagliari, and anchored safely within it.

A number of picturesque-looking boats soon put off to hail us; among them, one with the English consul, Mr. Bomeester, on board. Coming from Marseilles, which was infected with smallpox, we found we were liable to a quarantine of ten days! My husband, however, was allowed to meet the authorities of the town at the Parlatorio, and what with his representations, our intermediate purification at Bandol, and perhaps a little curiosity on the part of the natives to see an English family, we were admitted to *pratique* that evening. We took care to throw overboard the basket of dates given by the good-natured French officers, for had such a proof of communication with the East been found upon us, we might not have been liberated so easily. Once more, therefore, we thankfully found ourselves again on *terra firma*.

CHAPTER 5

Sardinia

Terra sana, e generativa.—Machiavelli.

In these days of modern travel and rapid motion, it is, perhaps, difficult to find a place which has not been visited and described by some of our nomade country-people. The "Grand Tour" of our forefathers, performed once in a man's life, through France, Switzerland, and Italy, by the aid of a heavy *berline* and relays of rope-tackled horses, is now taken as a walk by our young academicians during the long vacation. Russia, Turkey, and Greece, come within the compass of a summer tour; while the Hellespont is crossed, the seven churches of Asia (or their sites) are visited, and Jerusalem itself is the object of many an enthusiastic traveller. Persia, Thibet, and even the Celestial Empire, are invaded.

"Lands classical and sacred," become familiar to most of us; and the vast plains of "the Pampas" are traversed as a "ride." But while steam (like the old woman in the fairy tale) supplies us with seven-league boots, both by land and sea, to the most remote parts of the known world, there are still some places not far distant which appear to have been overlooked, and of these (until the interesting account published of it in 1827 by Captain Smith, E.N.) the considerable island of Sardinia may be said to have been one; and possessing, as it does, the advantages of easy communication with the Continent, the capabilities afforded by fine harbours, and the resources of great natural productions, its state of comparative barbarism is the more extraordinary.

The accidents of wind and weather, which I have already described, made me a visitor on its shores the year after Captain Smith's book was published; and as it renders any further description superfluous, I merely (as one of the few Englishwomen who have, perhaps, been in the island) offer a few remarks, made at the time, on its general appearance, and the society of Cagliari, which, through the kindness of the English consul (the late George Bomeester, Esq.[1]), I was enabled to make during a stay of sixteen days, while our storm-tossed vessel, under his able superintendence, was put into a state somewhat more seaworthy than that in which we had sailed from Marseilles.

The appearance of the town from the sea is striking. Built on a rising ground, the houses, which are large and constructed of stone, appear to stand on terraces, elevated one above the other, and crowned by the citadel in the centre, interspersed with patches of green; while orange and lemon trees, with their white blossoms and golden fruit (for it was late in November), gave agreeable relief to the whole. But, like many other southern towns, this favourable impression wears off on a nearer approach. The *casteddu*, or castle, the marina, which skirts the sea, *Stampace*, or Villa Nova, constitute the modern Cagliari, which contains about 30,000 inhabitants.

The citadel is strongly fortified; the streets leading up to it are so steep that no carriages are available, and walking is very fatiguing. However, from their being narrow, and the houses high, a "shady side" may always be found, except under a meridian sun; but the open gutters before the doors, and the clothes-lines extended amicably from one window to another, over the heads of the passengers, make a walk anything but refreshing to the senses. The court, nobles, and Sardes of distinction, dwell in the castle. The marina answers to our city, being (with the exception of the foreign consuls, who find it more convenient, and the arms of whose respective governments are rudely emblazoned over their *portes-cochères*) inhabited exclusively by merchants.

We were lodged in what, I suppose, was the first hotel of the place, and which was literally *open house* all the twenty-four hours. The first night, what between the fierce attacks of swarms of mosquitoes and *tanti altri*, and the perpetual whirring sound of the favourite game of

---

1. Mr. Bometster died a few years since from an attack of fever, incidental to the country, which carried him off in a few days, during the absence of his family in England. To the zeal and intelligence with which he discharged the duties of his situation for a period of four-and-twenty years, ample witness can be borne by all who visited Sardinia during that time; but, owing to his limited salary and the necessary expenses to which he was liable, he was unable to make any provision for his family. It is to be wished, in a country like England, that some means were provided for affording something more than a mere gratuity to the widows and orphans of those whose lives have been spent in faithful and honourable service, and whose death has been accelerated by the trying circumstances of their position.

morra in an adjoining room, sleep was out of the question, even to the most weary; and I was wondering what time these *meridionali* took to rest, but soon found it was a very different arrangement with them to what Alfred made it. At any time of the day or night, when he feels so disposed, and without any previous ceremony, the Sarde, wrapping his sheep-skin or cloak about him, and with no softer bed than a wooden bench or the floor, finds that "balmy sleep" which is ofttimes denied "to a king."

The dinner-hour in Cagliari is two o'clock, and to this meal it is not the fashion to invite ladies; but, with the thermometer at 92° in the shade, I thought it "a custom more honoured in the breach than the observance," and I was quite satisfied only to join in the evening parties given by the authorities, out of compliment to our consul, who, with his amiable wife, appeared to be greatly respected by all ranks. The tables, I was told, were loaded with all kinds of native and foreign delicacies. What I saw of the cooking appeared to me too rich and heavy for our English taste, though the wild-boar, dressed with the *agro dolce* sauce (a happy combination, as it name implies, of sweet and acid), and a sort of cream, made of eggs and wine, called *sanbaion*, might be approved of by Monsieur Soyer himself.

The native ladies are very ignorant, hardly ever looking into a book; and their conversation turns upon nothing but dress, and the affairs of their neighbours, whom they watch from their windows the greater part of the day. Nor is the want of mental cultivation at all compensated for by their personal attractions. They are, generally speaking, about the middle height, heavy figures, and with complexions not dark, or olive, or even *tawny*, but positively *pale orange*! When full dressed, they wear seven petticoats (of six or seven breadths each) of the finest cloth, a rich scarlet or geranium colour, and bordered with gold or yellow. No stays, but a long binder of coarse calico confines the waist, and over it is worn a tight-laced bodice, with very full white sleeves. A little fantastic apron, and a veil thrown over the back of the head and falling on the shoulders, completes a costume which would be becoming to any but a Sarde beauty.

The dresses of the people are very picturesque, every trade being distinguished by a different one. That of the butchers is particularly handsome, and on a gala day is worth from £50 to £60 of our money, from the quantity of silver lace and buttons with which it is adorned: many of these descend from father to son. The shepherds wear dressed skins, with the fur or wool outside, made into a sort of tunic, with a scarlet *berretta*, or cap. Many of them carry a very long gun; and all the peasantry go armed with a sharp knife, stuck in the girdle, which is too often used in their frequent and seldom bloodless quarrels amongst themselves; but a stranger, and particularly an Englishman, is in no danger, except, indeed, in travelling through the country, he should go to the inns, instead of availing himself of the accommodation of the private houses that lie in his road—an impeachment of his hospitality which the irascible Sarde could not easily forgive.

The country abounds with game; they have no pheasants, but partridges, snipe, woodcocks, hares, quails, &c. &c., and last, and least, though not *least good*, thrushes, which feed on the myrtle-berries, and are dressed with the trail like woodcocks. One morning a *manzoni*, or flamingo, was sent us as a present: it measured exactly six feet from the tip of the beak to the end of the claw, and the plumage was from the palest shade of pink to the deepest geranium. These beautiful birds congregate in flocks of some hundreds, but are very difficult to get near: their movements, when seen from a distance, resemble a regiment of soldiers, and they advance in regular columns, with skirmishers sent on before, as if to reconnoitre.

The prickly pear, a specimen of which may be seen in the print of the Costume d'Ossieri, grows abundantly through the island. Taken out of the thick husk in which it is enclosed, and put into the coldest water before it is sent to table, it is rather a refreshing fruit; but woe be to anyone who attempts to gather it without being sufficiently defended against the almost imperceptible thorns which guard its leaves, and which are so easily detached, as to give rise to the idea that they are drawn out by mere attraction. To *take* them out is impossible; but, through that beautiful provision in nature, by which the bane and antidote are so often found together, a handful of earth rubbed in, will immediately remove them.

We went one day to the museum: the birds are ill-preserved, but the fishes are beautiful, and the collection of minerals very fine. Quantities of coral and some rare shells are found on the coast; and we saw one specimen of the *Pinna nobilis*, with a tuft of fine silky hair hanging from it, about fifteen inches long, and were told they sometimes reached twenty-seven inches. Gloves have been manufactured of this beautiful material; but they would be, as Queen Elizabeth said of the first woven silk stockings that were presented to her, "marvellous delicate wear." Various ores and precious stones, particularly amethysts, emeralds, beryl, and topaz, are found in the mountains, but the mines have never been worked to bring in the return they might do.

The kindness of General Roberti, the military governor, having placed his carriage at our disposal, we drove out one evening with the Consul and his lady, to the village of Quartù, about four miles from the capital; the surrounding villages within a certain distance being thus called Quintù, Decimù, &c. &;c. Being the afternoon of a saint's day, the congregation were just coming out of church as we arrived. Human skulls and thigh-bones are imbedded into the atrium and walls of the churchyard, a decoration not uncommon in Sardinia. The women walked along, not with the stately grace of the Spanish matrons, but with their hands folded stiffly before them, and looking neither to the right nor left, with very much the air of performing penance.

We drove to the house of one of the principal formers, which consisted of a great number of rooms, all on the ground-floor, opening into a wide corridor, which looked upon a large court. The servants were pursuing their different household occupations, superintended by the *padrona*, and three or four grownup daughters, one of whom was to be married in a few days: I was sorry not to be able to see the ceremony, which was to be on a scale corresponding with the wealth of the parties; but we were shown the *trousseau* and the rooms which were prepared for the young couple. The children and single people in a family never sleep but, on the floor, so that few beds are to be seen, and they are covered with brocade in a way that looks more gorgeous than comfortable, with fine embroidered pillows, edged with lace, laid on the outside.

The "*Uomo e Donna Campidanese*" in the print[2] are a newly-married couple just returning from church, in all their wedding *galanteria*. This ceremony, as well as that of the previous courtship and betrothal, are well described by Captain Smith, whose interesting book I would recommend to anyone who wishes for a further account of this curious people.

One room we looked into was quite perfumed by the large clusters of the grape, of which the Malvasian wine is made, which were hanging up to dry: in this state they will keep the whole winter, and, with the very sour bread made in the country, they form a principal article of food.

The *Campidano* is generally understood to mean the large plain

2. The publication of the sketches intended to accompany this little volume has been unavoidably delayed; should it ever reach a second edition, they will appear.

between Cagliari and Oristano, but is applied to other fruitful tracts in different parts of the island. Ozieri and Sassari, of which costumes are given, are of the number of these, Gallura is a mountainous district, and Alghero, the walls of which are seen in the print, is a fortified town, founded early in the twelfth century, by the Doria family, and afterwards given up to the Spaniards. Charles V. was so fond of this place, as to have contemplated making it his residence; and I was told that a strong remnant of the language and manners of Catalonia are still retained in the society of Alghero, an improvement, I should imagine, on the less courtly manners of Cagliari, for which Mr. Bomeester prepared me by saying, "You must not be surprised at one very common topic of conversation—fleas"!! and certainly I had not been many days in Sardinia before I ceased to wonder at it, if it be natural to speak of what is perpetually before you. In such myriads are these sprightly insects, that Mrs. Bomeester told me, whenever she paid a round of visits to the Sarde ladies, she always changed her dress in an empty room before she returned to her own apartments!

The Sardinian horses, like the Calabrian, are small, black, very spirited, and fleet, and we flew over the ground, on our return from Quartù, at something very like railroad speed. For riding they are broke into what is called the "*passo portante*," which, from the peculiar motion it gives the animal, requires the rider to have some practice in it before he finds it easy, and I am told that it is then considered less fatiguing than the natural paces.

When we arrived at home we went to the theatre, which was about to be closed for Advent. The house was small, and the performance nothing remarkable, either for music or acting. We spent one evening at the French Consul's, whose house was kept by his two sisters. There were several of the Sardinian nobility present; dress among the ladies, and the chase among the gentlemen, were the chief topics of conversation. Italian is spoken among the higher classes, though it is not the "*lingua Toscana in bocca Romana*." The lower ranks speak only Sarde, which is a sort of patois composed of Greek, Arabic, and bad Italian, and it is remarkable that many of the customs and manners, particularly in the interior and towards the north of the island, are exactly similar to. those mentioned by the old Greek and Roman writers.

A walk through Cagliari in the evening is most amusing to a stranger. The absence of lamps in the *piazzas* and streets is compensated for by numerous little fires in all directions, at some of which chestnuts are roasting, at others coffee is preparing, while the cries of the vendors and the various dresses of the picturesque groups which surround them, their dark eager faces lighted up by the bright glare of torches or of the sweet-scented and crackling wood-fires, form a *tableau vivant* sufficiently amusing to a stranger.

Our own northern clime affords many beautiful daylight pictures, but for *nocturnal* scenery (if I may so term it) we must go to the south: who that has ever seen it can forget the brilliancy of an illumination on the eve of some favourite saint (St. John and St. Paul, for instance), in Malta, where the numerous churches, traced in lines of light by thousands of coloured lamps, are reflected in the calm sea below; or the exquisite nights in lovely Italy, where myriads of glancing fire-flies seem to rival in numbers and brightness the starry orbs in the blue firmament above?

One of the principal comforts of life—water—is scarce and dear in Cagliari, being brought in from the country in casks, by mules, swung across a rough saddle, and the *"venditor d'acqua"* has a never-failing trade; though this limited supply, in so hot a country, and where most descriptions of tormenting insects abound, would be severely felt by a people less thick-skinned and more cleanly than the Sardes. Let me not, however, leave their island without gratefully acknowledging not only the valuable assistance of our own consul, but the kind attention of all the principal native inhabitants. A field-day was given in honour of the English officer who had been unexpectedly thrown upon their hospitality: every day there was a succession of dinners, *soireés*, and and musical parties, at the General's, the Governor's, &c. ; and our visit concluded by witnessing the splendid fireworks on the festival of Santa Barbara[3], the patron saint of the Artillery, when the whole town was brilliantly illuminated.

Loaded with presents of fruit and wine from our new friends, we sailed the following day for Malta, hoping to arrive in about twenty-four hours; but *l'homme propose et Dieu dispose,* and before we reached our destination we had reason more than once to wish ourselves back, in spite of *sirocco,* mosquitoes, &c. &c., among the wild, but hospitable, inhabitants of Sardinia.

---

3. The following invitation was sent us for this *festa,* the previous day:—

"*Il Corpo Reale Artiglieria, celebrando l'annua festa dell' invitta martire sua Protettrice Santa Barbara, nella Chiesa di Santa Caterina Vergine Martire, prega V. S. Illma d'intervenire per la messa solenne e benedizione del SS. Sacramento, che avrà luogo in detta chiesa.*

"*Il 10 Decembre, alle ore 10½ del mattino.*"

CHAPTER 6

Malta

"Les fortifications étaient si formidables, qu'un général Français, en les examinant, s'écriait, dans sa franchise militaire: 'Il est bien heureux qu'il se soit tronvé quelqu'un là-dedans pour nous ouvrir les portes, car nous n'y serions jamais entrés tout seals.'"—Vertot: Histoire des Chevaliers de Malte.

It was on the 11th of December that we embarked for the third time for Malta. The kind consul and his wife accompanied us on boards and only left; us when we weighed anchor in the afternoon. The cases of tin, which had caused us so many unlucky tumbles in the first cabin, had been sold, to defray the expenses of putting our vessel into better condition; some things had been added for our comfort; the breeze was favourable, and once again *Hope told a flattering tale,* as we gradually lost sight of that wild shore where we had been so hospitably received by those who never knew of our existence till we were unexpectedly thrown upon their kindness, and whom we were never likely to see again.

Our first point was to be Maretimo, to the south-east of Sicily, which we expected to "make" in the course of the night after we left Sardinia. My husband, whose confidence in our crew was considerably shaken, had remained late on deck, and was fortunately on the lookout, when he thought he perceived breakers ahead. The captain was gone quietly to his hammock, having allowed us to get forty miles out of our reckoning, and we were actually just off the island of Ustica, almost near enough to have jumped from the bow-sprit on the rocks! With the help of the only sailor on deck—the only one, indeed, who knew anything of his business—he succeeded in getting the vessel about, and in the course of a few hours we were under the lee of

Sicily; happy for us that we were so, for in a little time a more violent storm than any we had yet experienced began to blow, and, I suppose, in no sea do they get up more rapidly than in the Mediterranean.

The waves ran mountains high; we really appeared *to mount into the heavens, and go down into the deep,* and it seemed next to a miracle that we were not engulfed in those mighty waters, when, leaving the shelter of the land, we crossed the channel which divides Sicily from Malta. The twenty-four pounders on one of the batteries in the latter were dismounted and thrown into the sea, like so many pop-guns, by the violence of this *gregale* (the Euroclydon of St. Paul), and several naval officers, who were watching our little craft from her first appearance in the horizon, declared it to be "next to impossible that she could ever reach the shore."

As we neared the island I was told, afterwards, that our keel was occasionally completely out of the water; and it was some time after we were safely anchored in the great harbour, on the *forty-third* day after leaving Marseilles, before I could realize our signal deliverance: even there the swell was so considerable, that when we landed in the evening, we were obliged to seize the moment to spring from the boat on to the marina before the receding wave carried it back again. As the time we had left Marseilles was known, and no tidings of the *Susan* had been heard in the interim, it was fully believed we had perished in the storm, and the unexampled *contretemps* of our voyage had excited a general feeling of interest in the island.

Rooms had been engaged for us at Beverley's hotel; and after all we had gone through, Valetta, as I first saw it, on a clear moonlight night, the large balconies and verandahs flinging their long shadows across the streets, appeared to me a city of palaces. Tea was waiting for us by a blazing fire, and, *pour comble de bonheur,* there lay on the table a large packet of English letters, the first we had had for weeks. It would be difficult to describe the happiness of that night. I could hardly go to bed for fear of losing, in sleep, the consciousness of our safety; and yet it was worth sleeping, for the joy of waking to the reality;—a luxury like that of the old general officer, who used to make his servant wake him every morning, saying, "Sir, the parade waits," for the pleasure of turning round and going to sleep again.

Malta, geographically and historically, is too well known to need any description; my *Recollections* will be confined to a slight sketch of the island, and its society, during part of the time the late Sir Frederic Ponsonby was governor there; and perhaps few men were ever more beloved in that situation, combining, as he did, with the manners of a high-bred gentleman, the greatest modesty of character and the most cultivated intellect. This gallant officer was known through the army, in which he served with such distinction during the Peninsular war, by the name of the "British Platoff." Charging at the head of his regiment, the 12th Light Dragoons, Sir Frederic Ponsonby was left for dead on the field of Waterloo, and was there ridden over by a body of the enemy's cavalry. A French soldier, who saw him on a heap of slain, actually planted his musket upon him and was about to fire, when he perceived some symptoms of life, and, applying a little flask of brandy to his mouth, revived him. Sir F. Ponsonby afterwards found out in Paris the man who had thus providentially been the means of saving his life.

It is a very pleasant thing, on arriving in a new country, to find not only the necessaries and luxuries of life so much cheaper than one has been accustomed to, but likewise, that every half-crown goes as far as three shillings. Every Maltese penny contains twelve grains, and it was amusing enough to see the twelve different things that might be bought for a penny, in the market at Malta. House-rent, which is always paid one quarter in advance, is exceedingly moderate; for our first house, in the Strada Reale, we paid twenty-three pounds *per annum*. It was built in the usual style of Maltese houses, round a court, with a well in the centre; an open staircase led, by a flight of fifty steps, to a drawing-room, nearly forty feet long, and thirty more to the terraced roof above.

Furnishing was a very easy matter: our dining-room tables cost 13s. 4d., chairs 1s. 8d. each; sofas 10s. Two or three Maltese women, who worked for 6½d. a day, soon covered the latter, and, picking to pieces some ropes of Indian grass, stuffed mattresses, quite equal in coolness and comfort to any made on elastic wires. Over iron bedsteads are thrown clear musquito net curtains, and if, in destroying these nightly tormentors with the flame of a candle, they should be set on fire, the mischief does not extend far on the stone or *puzzolana* floors. A story was told of a gentleman, who had lived many years in Malta, and who was in the habit of reading in bed: one night his curtains caught fire, he quietly walked into the next room to finish his sleep on the sofa, and desired the servant, on coming in the next morning, to "go into the adjoining room and sweep up the ashes."

The cooking in Malta is done by men. The kitchens, which are generally underground, are furnished with a few earthen vessels, many of them resembling in shape the old Etruscan jars and vases. The fire is in small stoves of the same material, and is fanned with large flat "*ventagli*," made of matting; and there can hardly be a greater difference than between the simple necessaries of a Maltese kitchen, and a *batterie de cuisine* in England. Our breakfast hour, in summer, was between seven and eight; dinner from three to four, and all the visits were paid afterwards.

The weather is often cool till towards the end of May, and nothing can be more beautiful than the lovely moonlight nights in July, when we used to drive out to the different villas in the country. A flag is hoisted where people are disposed to receive; and those garden parties, with geranium hedges, and avenues of oleanders, lighted up with coloured lamps, used to remind me of the descriptions in the *Arabian Nights*, of oriental entertainments.

The *calesse* is a carriage peculiar to Malta, and is generally drawn by small Barbary horses, and driven by a bare-footed *Smiche*, who, tightening his parti-coloured sash or girdle about him, will keep up with the animal at full trot, without any apparent fatigue. At first, this struck me as a very uncomfortable arrangement, but custom soon reconciles one to anything; though I did not quite agree with a lady, who assured me "it was quite *constitutional* to the *calessieri* to go at this pace;"— reasoning worthy of Mrs. Malaprop, or the cook who skinned the eels, and said "they were accustomed to it."

The summer palace of St. Antonio was built by the Grand Master De Paula, who was determined to choose a site from no part of which the sea was visible. Being inland, and rather low, it does not come in for the breeze which is so refreshingly felt in most parts of the island, and which has made it, not unaptly, compared to a ship at sea. The gardens, however, are extensive and beautiful, and, when watered in the evening, the fragrant perfume from the various tropical plants which are cultivated there is delicious. Among other plants, the Japan *medlar* flourishes in great perfection: it is like a large *magnum-bonum* plum in appearance, but of a much finer flavour, and very juicy; every variety of melon, fig, grape, pomegranate, and pineapple abound; the only fruit which looked miserable, and yet upon which the greatest care had been bestowed, were some common currants and gooseberries!

The system of irrigation is very well practised in Malta; there are wells in all the gardens, with a double set of buckets, two of which rise as the others descend, and the water is conducted from them into long, narrow channels, which lead to trenches dug round all the principal fruit-trees. The climate of Malta in general is very healthy, and malaria is confined to some localities without any apparent cause: in the deserted village of St. Paolo it may be accounted for, from the vicinity of some marshy ground; but the same reason does not apply to a house we frequently passed, standing in the middle of another village by the roadside, which had been for years uninhabited, or to a country house on the coast, belonging to the governor, towards the north-west of the island. People have gone there prepared against infection, others without knowing the character of the place, and upon whom, therefore, fancy could have no influence; but all, more or less, have been affected.

The arrival of the packet from England is an event of much interest in Malta, and when it is expected many an anxious eye is turned to the signal station at Fort St. Elmo. At last the well-known ball and flag appear;[1] the loungers on the ramparts and bastions turn their steps to the projecting point, which must be passed, at the entrance of the great harbour. The vessel, if not "big with the fate of Caesar and of Rome," is at least of equal moment "to all whom it may concern," drops anchor, the little boat with the mail-bags shoots across the water, and a few minutes afterwards the post-office is besieged, until the letters are sorted and delivered. Then for a time the streets are deserted, and when groups again appear, it is to discuss public news, and communicate private intelligence; and often enough at church, the Sunday following, the mourning garb of some shows that the packet has brought "a mingled yarn" of joy and sorrow.

In the autumn of this year (1829), died Leo XII., Annibale della Gruga.[2] He had been six years in the pontifical chair, and was a man of liberal principles; it was even hinted that he died a Protestant! Masses, however, were ordered for the repose of his soul, and he was buried, in effigy, with much pomp, in the great church of St. John. The exterior of this church is very plain; the interior is still beautiful, though deprived by the French of many of its treasures. Some of the lateral chapels are exquisitely finished, and rich in gilding and sculpture, and the pavement is a beautiful mosaic of different coloured marbles, intermixed with agate and jasper. The hand of St. John, the patron saint, is shown on high festivals, but having seen the duplicate right arm at Siena, and heard of many others (though never but of one Briareus), I

1. These signals were used in the time of the Order, and have been continued ever since.
2. Born at Cesena, a small town eighteen miles south of Ravenna

72

leave this point to the faith or credulity of my readers.

The Governor's palace (once that of the Grand Master) forms one side of the open space called St. George's Square. There are some splendid apartments on the first floor, to which you ascend by so gradual a flight of stairs, that on public occasions the knights used to mount them on horseback, in full armour. The library contains their literary treasures; and in the armoury, which is above two hundred feet long, are still contained many suits of their armour—some of them inlaid with gold. In St. George's hall the state balls are given. A band of white marble, on which are inscribed the signs of the Zodiac, traverses this beautiful room, and it requires some little care to waltz safely over this treacherous ecliptic. A ball was given on the 9th of June, in honour of Marshal Maison, who came out of quarantine, and who had the good taste to admire particularly the Rifle uniform, at the review in the morning. I could not return the compliment to one of his officers, who danced all night in his cap, an immense heavy *shako*, with an upright feather in front.

The palaces of the Knights are now converted into officers' barracks. The Rifles were quartered in that of Bavière, once d'Angleterre, when England had her knights among the eight languages or orders of St. John of Jerusalem. They were suppressed by Henry VIII., partially restored by Mary, and in the reign of Elizabeth their lands were finally confiscated, and the name of their *albergo* changed to that of Bavière. The last of the old knights was still living when we were in Malta, and used to wander about, a shadow of departed greatness. He was of a noble French family, and had been, in early youth, page to the Grand Master Hompesch. I remember Lord Prudhoe (who spent a few days in Malta on his way from Egypt) telling us that it was worthwhile knowing him, to hear French spoken in its purity.

Poor old Carlo di Grische! I used to think it was sad to see him, the last of his race, upon his own ground, and yet, probably, of less importance than the youngest drummer in the garrison. In winter he always wore a pale apple-green coat, trimmed with white fur; in *summer,* one of bright scarlet. He told me he had been sixty years in the island, and never seen snow but once; hail is more common, and I have seen heavy storms as late as May. Hurricanes have severely visited the "*Fiore del mondo*" (as the Maltese call it) at different times: one, in 1554, upset the vessels in the harbour, and shook St. Angelo on its strong foundations; and during a second, which happened within the memory of man, a sentry was carried out in his box into the sea, but was afterwards rescued from his ticklish position, and brought safe to land.

Thunder and lightning are frequent towards the end of the year, and the Maltese have a great dread of these autumnal storms, and set the bells ringing as hard as they can, to disperse the clouds and drive away evil spirits. The great bell in the church in the Strada Forni was powerful enough, as far as noise went, to do both. The hours of the day are not counted, like the Italian, to the *venti-quattro,* but as ours are, from twelve at noon to twelve at night. In the very hot weather all business, is suspended during the middle of the day; every Maltese takes his *siesta,* and even the English soldiers are sent to their beds. The heat is great, but most overpowering during a prevalence of *scirocco* wind, which generally blows during great part of September, from the south. It is, however, a useful scapegoat for all sins of omission or commission. If your Maltese servant is more than commonly careless; if your toast be burned and the coffee thrown over; if glasses and plates be broken, and your dinner utterly spoiled—"*è tutto quel maladetto vento di scirocco.*"[3]

We witnessed one curious phenomenon connected with this wind while we were in Malta: for two days the air was as thick as London in a November fog, and everything was covered with the finest red sand. This, in a climate where for months together the sky is without a cloud, greatly alarmed the superstitious Maltese, who thought the end of the world was coming. In peculiar states of the atmosphere, Mount Etna is visible to the naked eye; I saw it twice very clearly defined against the horizon; the last time, which was a lovely May evening, it appeared to be of a beautiful rose-colour. The channel which divides the islands is sixty miles wide, and from the shore to the mountain is about the same. The view at all times from the terraced roofs is varied and interesting. The busy town below, with its numerous churches and palaces and public buildings; the three deeply-indented harbours, full of the shipping of all nations; on one side the island gradually rising to the ancient capital, Città Vecchia, and on the other the blue Mediterranean, with the little mosquito fleets of fishing-vessels, and the light *sparonaras,* starting for, or coming in from Sicily,—and all under such a sky, that, as a lady who had lived many years in the island once said to me, "one really feels that existence alone is a blessing."

We used often in the evening to go down the famous "*Nix mangiare*" stairs, of which Lord Byron says, "*how surely he who mounts them swears,*" and, taking boat from the Marina, go round the harbours and visit our friends in the different ships: the *Britannia* (which had been

3. Wine, bottled during the time this wind is blowing, is quite spoiled.

the flag-ship at Plymouth), the *Prince Regent, Windsor Castle, Revenge, Asia*[4,] *Melville, Ganges, Blonde, Spartiate, Madagascar,* and many others, formed part of the squadron in the Mediterranean at this time. One evening, when we were alongside the *Melville,* we found the first lieutenant just preparing to join the *Prince Regent,* lately arrived from England, with the Admiral, Sir Henry Hotham, on board, and offered to convey him in our boat. He was greatly beloved in his old ship, and no sooner was he seated, than in a moment the yards were manned, and the sailors gave him three cheers: the man who would have braved death at the cannon's mouth was fairly overcome by this unexpected and simultaneous tribute of affectionate goodwill.

The garrison races used to be held on the Pietà, a broad road which skirts the sea at that extremity of the quarantine harbour which runs up into the land. The officers rode their own horses, and as the balconies used to be full of spectators, and the water covered with boats, it was a very gay sight. Mr. Freere's house was always thrown open on the occasion, and a ball was generally given somewhere in the evening.

One of Lady Error's *protegées* was a beautiful Greek child, who had been rescued in a massacre in one of the islands, and brought to Malta; she was too young to remember her parents, or any particulars of her early life, more than a confused remembrance of lying on the ground, and seeing horses' hoofs prancing over her! The Greek women are eminently beautiful. I remember three in Malta who could hardly be surpassed in their different styles. One of them, the wife of a merchant, had been brought up at *Constantinople,* and was on. her way with her husband to *Manchester.* How she bore the transition from the "Sublime Porte" to that city of factories I never heard.[5]

---

4. A ball was given one night on board the *Asia,* by Captain H. I., in honour of his wife's birthday; the boats belonging to the ship were in waiting all night conveying the guests backwards and forwards. The main deck, covered in with flags, made a beautiful ballroom; the cabins were all thrown open, and supper was laid out on the quarter-deck. It was something quite new in the way of a ball, and the only damp to our amusement was an accident which happened to one of our party (an officer on his way home from India), the heel of whose boot shot off the slippery landing-place as he was getting into the boat, and down he went into the water; he was soon got out again, but too completely drenched to do anything but return to his hotel and to bed.

5. The Greek patriarch in Malta was one of the finest-looking men I ever saw; he was considerably more than six feet high, with a beard that reached down below his girdle, and was often to be seen in his long flowing robes walking about the town, one of the many picturesque-looking figures in this motley place.

More or less, I suppose, all are liable to "skyey influences," but it is only those who have lived in the south who can understand the magical effect of climate on the feelings, where sunny days are succeeded by cloudless nights;—

Where the tints of the earth and the hues of the sky,
In colour though varied, in beauty may vie,
And the purple of ocean is deepest in dye;—

and I have often thought that instead of the constitutional melancholy the Englishman is accused of, he must have the greatest portion of animal spirits, to be enabled to resist the heavy pressure of fog and damp our island is exposed to. The influence of the sun is *tasted* in the deliciously ripened fruits of Malta. Oranges are in perfection in December;—flowers and fruit on the same branch. Those that are gathered for exportation are packed before they are ripe, and it is only the common kinds that bear the passage. The blood or red orange of Malta (procured by grafting a slip of orange on a pomegranate stock), though very fine, is not in flavour or size to be compared to the egg-orange, so called from its oblong shape. The highly-perfumed little mandarin orange is never, I believe, taken out of the island; the rind is extremely fine, and almost comes off with a touch, when ripe.

The small apricot (*Alessandrino*) is called "kill John" by the Maltese, from the quantities said to be eaten by the English. The *fichi di San Giovanni,* which ripen about the 24th of June, are the first of their kind; the luscious purple fig, its saccharine juice bursting the skin, comes in later; then there is the exquisite white nectarine, the cooling pomegranate, and the refreshing water-melon, while grapes are really "as plenty as blackberries." Vegetables, also, are abundant and excellent; we used to have salads and green peas in December, and say it was worth the voyage only to eat the potatoes.

Every spot of ground is cultivated: wherever an artificial soil can be created, there the industrious Maltese will set his potatoes, or put in early vegetables, and the numerous terraces supporting the earth cause the island to have a totally different aspect according to the point you see it from. Looking *up* to Città Vecchia, one sees nothing but lines of stone walls, but *down* from thence it appears to be covered with a verdant carpet. In none of the gardens is vegetation more luxuriant than in the ditches, from the shade they are in during great part of the day. On the walls the beautiful caper-plant grows in great abundance, its long wreaths of lilac blossoms covering the face of many of the outworks. A few years since an order emanated from the Ordnance, that "no one was to be allowed to *cut capers* on the bastions, except the commanding officer of Engineers," and it has ever since remained his distinctive privilege.

Almost forgetting in this climate the succession of the seasons, I was surprised one morning, on looking out of my window, at seeing the street full of people, dressed in every variety of colour and fancy, and all masked. It was the first day of the carnival, which fortunately only lasts during three—long enough for people to outdo each other in every species of buffoonery. On the second day every carriage in the place is in requisition, and down the long Strada Reale and up the Strada St. Paolo a moving line is formed; and as every window must be down to escape being broken, you are fairly exposed to "the pelting of the *sugary* storm."

The last day, the officers, in the armour of the old Knights, had a tournament in St. George's Square, and it was rather amusing to see these mailed warriors, when unhorsed, requiring assistance to get on their legs again. I do not think there was any "queen of love and beauty" on this occasion; but, *en revanche*, the Knights were not obliged, as at the Eglinton tournament, to fight under umbrellas!

The next morning all the churches were open for the sprinkling of ashes; the women resumed their *faldettaa* and black petticoats, and the men returned to their usual occupations. Lent is strictly observed by the Maltese, and Easter as joyfully commemorated. The custom of a man, divested of clothing, running from one end of the Strada Reale to the other at break of day, to typify the resurrection, has been some time discontinued.

Just beyond the Porta Bomb is the suburb of Floriana; the public gardens form a square in the centre. Here, among many curious plants and shrubs, is a thorn, said to be of the same kind with which the Saviour's head was crowned: it is a species of *marrucca*, and certainly exactly the same as that represented in the pictures of the old masters. The houses in Floriana are still more reasonable than those in Valetta, and we paid for one, which had been previously occupied by Lord F., £16 8s. *per annum*! The terrace, shaded by a vine-covered trellis, commanded a view of the great harbour, with its numerous and ever-varying naval population; of the dockyard, which occupies the place where the old galleys used to be built; of Isola, Brumela, the towering fortress of St. Angelo, the point of Ricasoli, the unfinished palace of Napoleon, and the line of forts which guard the eastern coast of the island.

It was an interesting and, generally speaking, very animated panorama; and the contrast was the more striking, when, one sultry evening
in June, the *Madagascar* was signalled from Alexandria with the dead
body of her captain, Sir Robert Spencer, on board, who, only ten days
before, had taken out the Governor-General, Lord Clare, on his way
to India. It was then a brilliant morning, the yards of all the ships were
manned, the Marina was lined with the troops, the "meteor flag of
England" waved in the breeze, and salutes were fired from the batteries
as the noble ship cleared the mouth of the harbour; but before a week
had elapsed Sir Robert had fallen a victim to fever, and, under the op-
pressive influence of a *scirocco* wind, the Madagascar now returned, her
white line painted black, like a moving coffin on the waters.

The colours were now all half-mast high, and minute guns were
fired from the batteries as the gloomy ship slowly swung round to
her moorings. Ten days she lay in quarantine. On the morning of the
eleventh the coffin was lowered into the captain's gig, and, followed
by the officers and all the ship's company, proceeded to the shore. The
troops of the garrison were drawn up to receive them; and the effect
of the whole, as (with arms reversed) they crossed the drawbridge,
and wound up through the fortifications, till they formed in funeral
order on the parade-ground of Floriana, the muffled drums playing
the Dead March in 'Saul,' as they moved on in slow time to the bastion
where "earth was to mingle" again "with earth," was very striking.[6]Sir
Robert Spencer was universally beloved and regretted, and every
demonstration of respect was paid to the memory of one who knew
how to combine the kindness of a friend with the discipline of the
commanding officer.

In the course of this autumn the squadron at Malta was ordered
to Naples, in consequence of the very unsettled state of the country,
where a strong revolutionary spirit existed. Much sensation was also
created in the island by an order coming out from England for a
considerable reduction in the government salaries, by which it was
calculated about £15,000 *per annum* would be saved in the colony.
Many changes took place in consequence, and some of our friends
who returned to England had almost as bad fortune at sea as ourselves.
The *Gloucester* was wrecked off the coast of Spain; and the Onyx, after
being driven nearly out to America, reached England after a passage

6. A pillar was erected to the memory of Sir Robert Spencer on the heights of
Coradino.

of eighty-four days: the longboat had been broken up for fuel, and the passengers reduced to a daily allowance of biscuit and water.

In spite of Lord Byron's abuse of "this little military hothouse," I never knew a place, for its size, possessing the endless variety of Malta. The influx from all parts of the world, of the merchant, the traveller, the soldier, and the sailor, keeps the island in a state of perpetual movement; and since Egypt, in fulfilment of the prophecy, has literally become "a high-road to the East," every variety of face, feature, and complexion, dress, language, and occupation, may be seen in the streets and in the harbours of Valetta.

Dr. Yeats, whose philanthropic devotion to the interests of science is well known, was there during our stay on his way to Egypt, to test, in his own person, the nature of the plague; the enterprising Sir John Pranklin, the venerable Lord Lynedoch, the young Prince de Joinville, the Prince of Salms, the talented author of *Vivian Grey*, the indefatigable Dr. Wolff, and many other people " of note," visited the island while we were there; and during the summer, a monthly steamer from Genoa and Naples brought a fresh importation of English tourists.

Malta was also a favourite yachting station; and I remember a characteristic anecdote of the owner of one of these vessels, a Captain Roberts, whose crew mutinied for increase of pay when about to sail from Genoa to Naples. Determined not to yield, he weighed anchor, and navigated his yacht down the coast. Off the harbour of Naples he received the usual challenge. "The name of the captain?"—

"Roberts."

"Of what did the crew consist?"—

"Roberts."

"Anyone on board?"—

"Roberts."

They lifted up their hands and eyes, exclaiming, "*è vero Inglese!*"

Dr. Wolff was in quarantine on his return from Persia, and before proceeding to Timbuctoo, in search of the lost tribes: to facilitate his progress up the country, it was necessary that he should allow himself to be sold as a slave, and he was then learning to shave. Of the fallacy of his views with regard to prophecy, Dr. Wolff was afterwards himself convinced; but the account of his adventures was very amusing, and the energy, patience, and courage, with which he surmounted hardships and difficulties were admirable. Lady Georgiana remained in Malta during the doctor's absence, and, hardly less enthusiastic than himself, took an active interest in the benevolent institutions of the island.

Besides the Casa d'Industria, which I have before mentioned, there was an excellent normal school, where work used to be taken in; shirts beautifully made at 6d. apiece, and other things on the same moderate terms. A committee of ladies was formed for the relief and employment of the poor, of which the indefatigable wife of Mr. Wilson, the missionary, was the secretary: about twenty poor people were given to the charge of each, and an account of the work done, and the money distributed, was rendered every month at a meeting held on purpose. "*Man wants but little here below;*" but *how* little that is, no one has an idea who is unacquainted with the life of the poor in a warm climate. Of fuel and clothing the least possible quantity suffices; a few beans fried in oil, a little *pasta* boiled in water, and coffee without either milk or sugar, form a principal part of the food of the poor Maltese. One old woman and her daughter, who were among my best knitters, had for years lived under no other shelter than the hollow space formed by a flight of stone steps!

The Maltese language is a dialect composed of Italian and Arabic. Many of their words have not the slightest resemblance to the former. "*Hops*" is *bread;* "*haleep,*" *milk;* "*jaubon,*" *cheese.* "*Hempshee maur,*" "*Go, I have nothing for you,*" is a phrase soon learnt in self-defence against the tribes of beggars who assail you at every step. Some English words they adapt in a curious way. Soon after we arrived in Malta, a native servant came one day and told me that "a John and two Mariannes were in the drawing-room." I went in, not knowing what to expect, and found Capt. P. B., his wife, and daughter! I afterwards found that these names are a sort of generic term among the Maltese for our country-people.

Unlike the Italian, the *natural* music of the Maltese (if I may so term it) is of the most inharmonious kind.[7] They have two or three native airs, the copy of which I have unfortunately lost. The opera in Valetta, while we were there, was very indifferent; an amateur play, which was got up by the officers, was much more amusing.

The fish-market, which is held in a projecting angle of the Marina, is well worth a morning visit. In the centre, on a raised flight of very broad steps, is a quadrangular stone basin, into which a fountain plays, and a figure of Neptune, one hand holding the trident and the other resting on a dolphin, surmounts the whole. All around are the ven-

---

7. The Scotch and Irish bagpipe is one of the common instruments in Malta; and we heard exactly the same in the district of Morven, near Autun, in France.

dors, in their picturesque costumes, selling no less picturesque-looking fish—many of curious forms and the brightest colours, but few, to an English taste, good to eat—the grand master, john dory, and red mullet, of course, excepted. The sea-horse *(Equus marinus),* so called from its resemblance to the head of that animal, is also found in the Mediterranean.

Horses are brought over from Barbary three or four times in the year, and these arrivals were always a matter of interest among the officers. They generally come in wretched condition, but soon improve with good food and grooming: they are small, but well made and spirited. The Maltese asses, or rather those from Gozo, are a very superior race to that we are accustomed to. Their colour is generally a very deep *brown,* almost *black,* and I have seen many fifteen hands high.

The little breed of dogs peculiar to the island is almost extinct. One was offered to me, but I could not bring it home: it was exceedingly small; black and white, soft and shining as silk. I never saw a full-grown dog like it in size, except one of a similarly miniature kind brought from New Mexico. The Gozo dogs were in great request among the Roman ladies, and, I think, must have been the originals of the present tribe of lapdogs.

The shops in Valetta somewhat resemble oriental bazaars, containing an *omnium gatherum* it would be hard to describe. There is no incivility among the shopmen, but an indifference to whether you purchase or not, which strikes those accustomed to the *(parfois)* officious civility of an English tradesman. If a thing does not suit you, they turn it over with a "come *vuole, Signora,*" and go on with some other occupation. The ships which are constantly coming down from the East bring an abundance of oriental luxuries—some for sale, and many presents from settlers or visitors in that part of the world. Brusa silk, Greek caps, drums of figs, and musk purses; Carabousa cups and filagree saucers; Persian rugs and Turkey carpets; Constantinopolitan tobacco-bags and otto of roses; not forgetting the highly perfumed cigars and cigarettes, and the pretty little amber mouth-pieces—all are to be had either *for love or money* in Malta.

From some friends who came overland from India, I had a canister of the finest tea from China; another of coffee from Mocha (the little, ugly, bad-shaped berries, which all connoisseurs know to be "real Mocha"); and a sepulchral vase from Luxor, which had contained—a lady's heart! It was in the form of a cinerary urn, of pale terracotta, and marked with hieroglyphics on the outside.

The public granaries are not among the least curious objects in Malta. They consist of a number of deep pits, hollowed out of the solid rock, and covered with large stones at the top, strongly cemented down with *puzzolana* to exclude the air. In one of these, which had been overlooked (on being opened after the lapse of centuries), the grain, with the exception of a little at the top, was found to be as fresh as possible. These subterranean granaries remind me of the catacombs at Città Vecchia, the old capital of the island. Many of them are now closed, but their ramifications are said to have extended about fifteen miles. The entrance is through the house belonging to the *rettore* of the college.

The view from the hill on which the Città Notabile is built commands the greater part of the island, with its indented coast and little bays. That of St. Paul is always pointed out, and I see no reason for giving up for Malta the honour of having received this great Apostle with "no little kindness." The expression, *"driven up and down in Adria,"* is the only, one that can warrant the supposition of its being Meleda, at the entrance of the Gulf of Venice; all the rest of the account corresponds much better with Malta, in whose harbour " ships from Alexandria" were accustomed to winter. The place "where two seas meet" is caused by a counter-current over a shoal not far from the bay; and all the traditions of the island, would seem to identify it as the Melita of the Acts:—few of even the small villages are without a *strada* or *piazza* St. Paolo,—without a church dedicated to him, or a festival held in his honour.

There is also in Ploriana the Strada *"Pubblio."* The possessions of this "chief man of the island," at the time of St. Paul's visit, were about Città Vecchia; and tradition says the cathedral was built on the place where his house once stood. We spent one summer in the country, at the Palazzo Guarena, belonging to our friend Colonel Morshead, of the Engineers. Built in an elevated situation, within half a mile of the sea, this villa was peculiarly adapted for a summer residence, and was known as the Palazzo dei Quattro Venti.

The entrance was into a large hall, where we used to dine, suspended to the ceiling of which was a *punkah,* to be used in hot weather while at table. Several rooms, appropriated to different household purposes, opened into this, and upstairs was a *saloon* in the form of a cross, the angles taken out of which formed four small bedrooms; glass doors on every side opened on to a broad stone terrace, which was carried round the building, and from which a flight of steps descended to the garden. Many a glorious sunrise and golden sunset we have watched from that terrace, from which the whole island lay like a panorama below, dotted over with castles and country-houses, the churches and palaces of Valetta in the distance, and the blue Mediterranean, covered with the ships of many nations, stretching away into the horizon.

Near to the house is a curious hollow, said by the peasants to have been made by the fall of a thunderbolt;[8] it is planted as a garden, and is most productive in vegetables. Our walks after sunset used to be delightful; sometimes we went to the fig-gardens, and while we ate the delicious fruit, our dogs used just as much to enjoy the rind as we pealed it off. Cotton is much cultivated in this part of the island, and at the time of gathering the pods, the groups of peasants in the fields, or returning home after the day's labour, had a very picturesque appearance. The flower and leaf of the cotton plant is not unlike that of the *Althea frutex*. There are three varieties: one a delicate primrose, another white, and a third of a pale tawny colour; and from the last the nankeen is manufactured, preserving the natural colour.

The watermelon also grows in great abundance in the fields, which are divided by low walls of loose stones, and every here and there the flat-topped acacia and the fan-leaved palm-tree give an oriental character to the landscape. I must not forget to mention, among the vegetable productions of Malta, the *Stila,* a species of cinquefoil, with a beautiful rose-coloured blossom, growing to the height of four or five feet, and containing so much saccharine juice, that the stalks, when of fire were celebrated, which is confirmed by some roughly-cut symbols still visible on the walls.

Another evidence of the larger size of the island at this period, I thought, appeared from the traces of a considerable road near the Torre dei Giganti, cut out of the solid rock. We measured the space intended for the wheels, and found the width to be exactly the same for some distance, and a work of this nature would be more likely to be carried on in a central situation, than just skirting the sea. The cliffs on this side, having some portion of magnesia in them, are liable to be affected by saline particles ; one cause of the decomposition constantly

8. The name of this place is Makluba, which signifies *overturned,* and the tradition is, that it was originally the site of a village, destroyed, like the "cities of the plain," for some signal wickedness. The country around is craggy and irregular, and bears the marks of having undergone some violent natural commotion. It is about one hundred and thirty feet deep, and the descent is by a narrow, rudely-cut flight of steps to the garden below.

going on.

We drove over one morning to the Inquisitor's Palace, where General and Mrs. B. were spending the summer. It is built at the head of a very rich valley, commanding a beautiful view. The garden, watered by a fine spring, produces an abundance of fruit, and, even in the heat of a July day, was verdant and fresh; the large and beautiful flowers of the *convolvulus major* hanging in graceful wreaths from one orange-tree to another, while, the miniature clusters of grapes on the Zante currant were covered with purple bloom, and many varieties of oriental shrubs and plants abounded; among the former, the *Palma Christi,* which grows to the size of a tree, flourishing in great luxuriance down the sides of the valley.

The drive back was partly through "the stony valley," a very remarkable ravine, immense stones lying in the wildest confusion; again reminding me of the enchanted city in the *Arabian Nights' Entertainments*. Whether they have been there since the creation, or caused by some violent concussion of nature, volcanic or otherwise, is not known. Emtahleb and Taura are also two fertile oases on this side of the island: both of them are watered by springs of fresh water, and produce quantities of fruit. These places are much resorted to by the Maltese on their *festas,* who lay out their dinners on the stone tables with which the gardens are provided.

The principal amusement in the way of sporting, for gentlemen, in Malta, is rabbit-shooting, in the little island of Cumino, half-way between Malta and Gozo, where parties used to go down to a house belonging to the Governor, for the purpose; and quail-shooting, of which there are two seasons, spring and autumn: the first *"passa,"* as it is called, ends on the 20th of May. Every flight of these birds is preceded by one of a larger size, with a tuft of feathers on the head, and a fan-shaped tail: this is called the king quail, and when shot is always reserved to be stuffed. The sportsmen are in the field by a little after four in the mornings and used to come in to breakfast with game-bags filled, but quite wet through, from the heavy dew on the ground at that hour, and to which providential supply of moisture the island is mainly indebted for its fertility. The *beccafico* is still smaller than the quail, very fat, and delicate in flavour, feeding, as the name implies, on the figs: and the Maltese always consider those the best which have been *pecked* by this bird; either instinct teaches them to select the best fruit, or they ripen more thoroughly from being thus opened to the sun.

The Boschetto is another favourite resort of the Maltese on gala days, and takes its name from the orange and lemon grove, which affords ample shade, while the golden fruit which strews the ground reminds one of the fabled gardens of the Hesperides. The palace, built by the Grand Master Verdala, has long been abandoned to silk-worms, and I believe they of late have been given up.

The principal historical interest in Malta is in the capital and in its forts, all of them the work of the Knights; but we found much to amuse us in the country, and in talking to the poor people, and hearing their tales (handed down from father to son) of the days of their island greatness. The memory of the Knights is held in much honour, that of the French equally detested; the present rule they seem to take as a matter of course, and on the whole they were, perhaps, never better off. They used to describe, also, the time when they were visited by the plague, in 1813. A vessel from the Levant, with bales of calico on board, put into the quarantine harbour.

All communication was forbidden with the shore; but a shoemaker in Valetta managed, by night, to smuggle some of the cargo, and convey it to his own house. Soon after this some of his family sickened and died, and wherever shoes had been sent home, there the plague appeared. The alarm now became general; all those who had villas in the country fled the town, thereby spreading the infection. There they remained for weeks, holding no communication with each other, and only venturing to breathe the air on the terraced roofs of the houses: in the entrance door of many of them I have seen the holes through which the absolutely necessary articles of food used to be put, and which were then passed through water. In the town no one stirred out but from the most urgent necessity, and then not without a passport from the Board of Health, and a cane, some feet long, held at arm's length, to prevent contact with any one they might meet. The mortality was dreadful among the Maltese; but few of the English, comparatively, were victims to it. It was said the disorder was communicated to Gozo through the cotton, on which some beads were strung, that had been sent over.

The customs and habits of the Maltese are very primitive, notwithstanding their long intercourse with other people. I always found them a most civil and obliging race, enduring fatigue and hunger very patiently, and grateful for every little kindness. Like most *meridionali*, they are passionate among themselves; but their rage generally evaporates in loud words and angry gesticulations. The women are particularly attached to the children under their care, and are tolerably amenable to English habits, though, when in the country, they will generally claim the privilege of going about barefoot. Caps, of course, they are never expected to wear; but they dress their long black hair in a very becoming manner.

The peasants in the country wear the old sandals, a piece of un-tanned bull's hide, fastened on the foot with thongs of the same; all wear the long *berretta*, or cap, a girdle three or four yards long, and their waistcoats fastened with the round silver buttons we had seen in Sardinia. The higher orders of the Maltese mix very little with the English. We knew the family of Count Rivarola, and one or two oth-ers; but in general they close their houses to strangers. Padre Andrea, the priest of our village, used often to pay us an evening visit, and fre-quently join us at dinner. *Sub rosâ*, I believe he was an excellent sports-man; he was a bit of a *virtuoso* also, and had a room filled with all kinds of curiosities, and was considered, by his flock, to go through a mass in shorter time than any of his neighbours! He was of very sociable habits, and I believe was very sorry when we left Crendi.

His parting gift was a couple of bottles of the most delicious Cy-prus wine I ever tasted, and some of the fragrant honey for which Malta is famous, and which derives its flavour, they say, from the flow-ers of the *Thymbra hirsuta*, which the bees feed upon. The plants, when gathered and dried, are tied up in bundles, and brought into the town for fuel, and with two or three of these a good fire is lighted up in a few minutes, and coffee is boiled.

The French revolution of 1830 happened about this time, and I re-member the excitement caused by the first ship that entered the har-bour with the tri-coloured flag at the mast-head. In the years which have since elapsed, these events, unfortunately, have been of too fre-quent occurrence to be much more than a *nine days' wonder*, however important they may have been in their consequences.

Our *villeggiatura* was now drawing to a close: the summer heat was over, during which time we had been enjoying a temperature 10° lower than that of Valetta; and the smallpox having been very bad there during that time, we had lingered on at the Palazzo dei Quat-tro Venti till near the end of November, when we returned to our winter-quarters at Floriana.

My next experience of life in Malta was at Fort Ricasoli, where my husband was ordered to take up his quarters soon after Christ-mas. This fort was built by the Cavaliere Gianfrancesco Ricasoli, during the Grand Mastership of Cottonera; he spent about £3,000 on the building, and endowed it with part of his fortune. The "Palace," which was to be our abode, contained but few rooms on the upper floor, which was all that was inhabited; but they were charming in summer,—cool, spacious, and airy, and with a north aspect. The dining and drawing-rooms, communicating by folding-doors, were 67½ feet long by 27 wide; a deep cornice round the latter, divided into compartments, contained the armorial bearings of the Knights who were in succession governors of Ricasoli; this was unfinished, and, as "the days of chivalry are past," it will probably remain so.

Six French windows opened on to a stone balcony, which ran the length of the building. This side looked into the fort, round which were the barracks occupied by the soldiers. Opening out of the dining-room were three or four other rooms, a door from one of them leading on to a bastion; and Fort Ricasoli being in the extreme angle of the promontory immediately opposite St. Elmo, the two forts guard the entrance of the great harbour. The fortifications are built on the solid rock, which goes sheer down into the water, and which is so deep there, that from our terrace we could speak to any one on board the largest men of war as they rounded the point.

One morning, the *Blonde* frigate, commanded by Sir Edmund Lyons, came in from the East, with every sail set; just off Ricasoli, the whistle was heard, and in a second she was under bare poles,—every sail furled, as if by magic,—a model of naval discipline. Fort Ricasoli was the scene of the revolt and dispersion of Froberg's regiment, in 1807, and is so strongly defended as to be almost impregnable by land as well as by sea. The artillery used to come over every week to practise the guns on the batteries, and if every window in the fort had not been thrown open, they would have been broken by the strong vibration. In fine weather, part of the squadron would stand out to sea, and give us the opportunity of watching a sham fight; and it was beautiful, when a broadside was fired, to see the masses of smoke rolling down the sides of the ships, and then curling away on the surface of the water, till the two elements became as one.

Many pleasant days we spent at the neighbouring fort, St. Angelo, where a friend of ours commanded a company of artillery. Four tiers of batteries face the sea; the highest forms a fine terrace, at one end of which is a little pavilion, quite overhanging the water. St. Angelo was the first place garrisoned by the Knights on their arrival from Rhodes, and the escutcheon and initials of L'Isle Adam, their Grand Master, is over a small doorway in the interior of the fort; that of Adrian de Wignacourt over the outer gate. The Sienite pillars in the little chapel are supposed to have been brought by the Knights.

Close to the chapel is a small garden within four walls, and the perfume of the oleanders, roses, jessamine, and gadsea used to be like that of a conservatory in full bloom. This last flower is a particular favourite with the Maltese, who stick the little raspberry-shaped blossoms on sprigs of thorn, and carry them about for sale; but the odour is so overpowering, I used to make it a *proviso* with our servants that they were never brought into the house, as they keep them with their clothes, &c.

Still farther up the harbour than St. Angelo is the garrison chapel; the troops attend here for divine service, as well as the officers connected with the dockyard. I was once there on the occasion of a christening: the clerk, who had been a soldier, came up, and almost unconsciously raising his hand to his head, asked one gentleman of our party, "All present, sir?" before the service commenced; in the same style of "military parlance" the hairdresser used to ask me whether I chose my hair "to be cut shorter in the rear:" so much can you judge of the general character of a place by the manners, and in the expressions, of the lower orders. This observation would occur to any one travelling in Prussia, where even in the villages the youngest subjects of the military Frederick form themselves into squares, and with brown paper caps, and sticks in their little hands, are drilling and exercising from morning till night.

Our favourite bastion at Ricasoli looked quite across the harbour upon the towns of Città Vittoriosa and Valetta: in a projecting bastion of the latter is the Greater Borraccha, a sort of promenade planted with trees, in the centre' of which is the cenotaph erected to the memory of Sir Alexander Ball, the first English Governor of Malta. We established a regular code of signals with our friends at St. Elmo, and when it was too rough to cross, we found it a very convenient mode of communication. We used often to walk beyond the line of forts which guard the north-eastern coast, and in the middle of winter would bring home bouquets of wild flowers, anemone, ranunculus, pheasant's eye, &c., which grow in the greatest profusion at this season.

Our fort was almost as well stocked as Robinson Crusoe's island with animals, which made us tolerably independent of supplies from without. There were only two "English dairies," as they used to be called, in the island, where the cows were kept by day in large subterranean stables, foddered down with the beautiful Sula and grass cut during the night, with all "the dew of the morning" upon it, and the butter made here was very good. Our goats supplied us abundantly with milk, and we had every description of poultry, besides dogs, donkeys, canaries, tortoises, &c. Rats, of course, abound in the ditches of all the forts, and the mice used to race over our beds at night, eat the bran out of the pincushions, and nibble the stalks of my beautiful balsams; and it was curious to see a party of them, if we opened the dining-room door half an hour after leaving the table, seated round if, discussing the crumbs, &c., on the floor, and on being disturbed, race up the long muslin curtains with as much ease as a rope-dancer.

There are few noxious animals in Malta, and I believe the useless experiment of introducing venomous snakes into the island completely failed. The centipede is a horrid black-looking reptile, between a worm and a caterpillar; and the wood slave, a species of lizard, but very disgusting in appearance, is found about old buildings, in walls and crevices, and being of a yellowish stone-colour, is not so easily detected. This animal has the power of contracting the foot, so as to make it very difficult to detach it from anything it has fixed itself on; the only way is to push it off by degrees. The scorpions are small, and not very venomous; the first I saw was picked up by one of my children in the balcony, not knowing what it was, and brought in to me as a curiosity.

Nothing could be more beautiful than the view from Ricasoli, on the eve of some great *festa*. The water below covered with boats, each of them with a light at the prow, many with music on board, to the cadence of which the rowers kept time with their oars; and above, the towns of Valetta, Borgo, and Burmola, with every church brilliantly illuminated. These illuminations do not consist in lighted windows, but every pillar, and cornice, and pediment is hung with little lamps, till the whole building appears to be traced in lines of living light, and the effect of this, reflected as it is in the dark blue sea below, is magically beautiful.

People abuse Malta, and call it a rock and a prison, and speak of the heat as unendurable; but I cannot help thinking there is *some* interest attached to a place which was the last stronghold of knighthood in Christendom;—not the degenerate knighthood of modern days, but of a race of noble birth, and bound by the rules of their order to the strictest purity of life and manners, who maintained their sea-girt fortress against the most formidable enemies, and only lost it through treachery: of a place, too, of sufficient naval importance to have been coveted and possessed successively by the Phoenicians, 1500 B. C, Greeks, Carthaginians, Romans, Arabs, Normans, Germans, French, and which for the last half-century has been one of the jewels of the British crown; and in that bright setting may it long remain!

The heat for some hours in the day during the summer months is certainly great, but it is more than compensated for by the lovely and cool moonlight nights; and except during the influence if a *sirocco* wind, there is always, once in the twenty four hours at least, that refreshing breeze from the sea which counteracts the effect of a hot climate on the system. In short, like the Irishman's idea of purgatory, "you may go farther and fare worse;" and even to return to England, I left Malta with regret. The opportunity, however, of a voyage in a man of war was not to be lost, and on the morning of the 31st of July we were putting off for the last time from the landing-place at Ricasoli, in one of the beautiful fourteen-oared boats belonging to the *Melville*.

The remainder of the day was spent in arranging our cabins and taking leave of the many friends who came on board to see us. The sorrow of our poor Maltese servants was quite overpowering. We weighed anchor in the evening, and when I looked out of my porthole the next morning, the sunny Ogygia of the ancients lay like a dark speck in the distant horizon.

CHAPTER 7

Graham's Island

With a rush,
Startling deep midnight on her throne, rose up,
From the red mouth of Etna's burning mount,
A giant tree of fire,—whence spouted out
Thousands of boundless branches, which put forth
Their fiery foliage in the sky, and showered
Their fruit, the red-hot levin, to the earth,
In terrible profusion. Some fell back
Into the hell from whence they sprang; and some,
Gaining an impulse from the winds that raged
Unceasingly around, sped o'er the main,
And, hissing, dived to an eternal home
Beneath its yawning billows.—Alaric Watts.

About ten days before we left Malta a new and extraordinary object of interest was occupying the attention of everyone in the island. The brig *Adelaide*, on her passage from London to Malta, reported having seen, at one o'clock p. m., on the 18th of July, a column of white smoke, rising out of the water, at a distance of about fifteen miles. This, after a time, changed into columns of black smoke, intermixed with flame like lightning, the surrounding water greatly agitated; latitude, about 37° 10' north; longitude, 12° 30' east.

This account, which was confirmed by the report of other merchant vessels passing in the same direction, excited a great sensation among the Maltese, who looked upon it as the precursor of some calamity, while the more enlightened part of the population were desirous of ascertaining the exact nature and situation of the phenomenon, which was of the more importance, being in the direct track of vessels coming from the N.W., midway in the channel of Malta, between Pantelleria and Sicily; and the *Philomel and Hind* cutter was accordingly despatched to make observations. In the meantime H. M. brig *Rapid*, Captain Swinburne, on her way from Marseilles, had seen the new volcano, and brought many additional remarks, made by her intelligent commander and officers.(See letter following.) Previous circumstances, frequently symptomatic of volcanic existence, had not been wanting, for on the eve of the 28th of June, when on the very spot where the island afterwards appeared, the Britannia and Rapid, in company, experienced the shock of an earthquake.

COPY OF A LETTER FROM CAPTAIN SWINBURNE
TO SIR H, HOTHAM.

H. M. S. Rapid, August 20.

Sir,—I have the honour to inform you, that in compliance with your order of the 18th of June last, I have examined the spot where the vulcanic island appeared last summer. It has left a dangerous shoal, consisting of black sand and stones, with a circular patch of rock in the middle, about 42 yards in diameter, on which there are 2 fathoms of water, but in one spot only 9 feet. All round the rock there are from 2½ to 3 fathoms, deepening gradually to 5 and 6 fathoms at the average distance of 100 yards from the centre: then more rapidly to 10, 20, and 30 fathoms. A small detached rock, with 15 feet on it, lies 130 yards S.W. of the central patch. About ¾ of a mile N.W. of the centre, there is a detached bank with 23 fathoms on it. All the rock appears to be dark-coloured porous lava, and the sand, which is extremely fine in the deepest water, is composed of particles of the same substance; by this the soundings near the shoal may be distinguished.

It should be approached with great caution, as a large extent of deep discoloured water, which lies to the S.W., may be mistaken for it, while the real danger is invisible till it is very near, being composed of dark-coloured materials, and it is so deep that the lead cannot be trusted. Its latitude and longitude are 37° 9—N., and 12° 43— E. of Greenwich. In four days, during which the wind was constantly from N.W., currents were perceived from N.N.W. and N.E., the N.W. prevailing, and sometimes running three-quarters of a mile an hour. The temperature of the water on the shoal does not differ from that of the sea at a distance. I have moored, in three fathoms water, at the N.W. of the shoal, a cask, painted white, with a pole surmounted by a white ball, and at the S.E. a similar cask, painted black, bearing a black ball on the pole. These two buoys are about 120 yards apart.

I have the honour to be, &c. &c.

The *Philomel and Hind* shortly after returned, with accounts varying only from the former as to the increasing size of the island; and Admiral (then Captain) Nesham determined to take it on his homeward course, and thereby gave us an opportunity of witnessing the sublime spectacle of a volcano in full eruption, rising out of the hitherto unbroken current of the ocean. No words of mine could ever do justice to the wondrous grandeur of the sight; I shall, therefore, merely describe my own impressions at the time, in which, I believe, I shall be fully borne out by all who were there present, many of whom had been in all parts of the world, and said this far surpassed anything of the kind they had ever seen.

It was on the 5th of August, at 6.30 p. m., smoke was first visible to the many anxious eyes on board the *Melville*, at the supposed distance of about thirty miles. This, as we proceeded, became more apparent, rising to a considerable height above the horizon; at first, as it appeared, from three sources, but further observation showed it to be but from one, divided by the wind, for presently another column arose to windward, whose more rapid ascent showed it originated immediately from the volcano, and which, as it settled over the water in a tardy progress to leeward, assumed a thousand picturesque forms. Bright forked flames were seen to dart upwards, and a loud rumbling noise was heard, compared by a young midshipman on board to the rattling of a chain cable when the anchor is let go.

At daybreak the following morning I was awoke by a rap at my cabin-door, someone telling me that we were fast approaching the island, and that I had better make haste, as we should soon have passed it, if the wind continued in the same direction. I made a rapid *toilette*, and, putting on my bonnet and cloak, ran upon deck; and never shall I forget the sublime sight! In the soft, warm, grey light of a Mediterranean morning, and from the bosom of a perfectly unruffled ocean, the new volcano was exhibiting its mighty operations. From the crater, which appeared in the form of a cone, jagged at the top, a fleecy vapour rose in globular clouds, which, expanding themselves majestically, assumed in their ascent the form of a towering plume—*si parva licet componere magnis*—that known as the illustrious decoration of the Prince of Wales.

Large stones, carrying with them a quantity of black dust, were thrown up, and, as they rose and fell, broke into a thousand curious shapes; and the effect of this, through the white vapour, was magically beautiful. Flashes, like lightning, darted occasionally through the vapour, and noise, as of thunder, was distinctly heard. All this time the white smoke was extending itself, so as to cover the whole island, hanging together like that which issues from Vesuvius, and then ascending in an unbroken column for a much longer time than smoke generally does. The eruption appeared to be most violent at intervals of two hours, and at 11.30 one took place in some respects different from those I have attempted to describe. It began with a similar burst of white vapour, and similar projections of stones and dust; but immediately after the latter followed a copious mass of black lurid smoke, which, overpowering the white vapour, covered in its turn the whole island.

The effect of this was less beautiful than the former, but more awful. At this time we were sufficiently near for the deck of the vessel to be covered with the black dust, which was thrown up in great quantities, and of which, as well as of some cinders, I have a specimen. It is harsh to the touch, and in colour resembles gunpowder. The latter were gathered in a curious way. The hides of some bullocks, which had been killed in the morning for the consumption of the ship, had been, as usual, fastened to the stern, to be purified by dragging through the water, and in them the cinders were entangled and brought up into the ship. The splash made by the stones which, during some of the eruptions, fell into the sea, at the estimated distance of about seventy feet from the island, was greater than that of a shot fired from an eighteen-pounder, and showed they must have been of considerable magnitude.

The wind was light, and the *Melville* made but little way. At one p.m., however, we passed the east corner of the island, when the immediate source of these eruptions was visible. Here was the mouth of the crater. On this side, the island, which in form resembled a horseshoe, with the sides somewhat beaten out, did not rise above the level of the sea, but formed a bay, and from this ebbed a boiling, bubbling stream, leaving its own track in the sea for about three-quarters of a mile. Here it seemed as if a continual conflict was waged between the two elements of fire and water. The sea, rushing into the mouth of the

94

crater, was opposed by the fire within, and, partly repelled, formed a whirling steamy Charybdis.

A volcano must always be an object of awe and admiration; but suddenly emerging from the sea, as this did, at the depth of 170 fathoms, it was indeed a sight never to be forgotten by those who had the good fortune to witness it. Every eye was on the island during that day; and to me the words of the Psalmist, in decribing the majesty of Jehovah, were perpetually recurring.

The Lord sitteth upon the water-floods, and the Lord remaineth a king forever.
At the greatness of his power his clouds removed, hail-stones and clouds of fire.

For six-and-thirty hours we were within sight or hearing of this grand phenomenon, but it was between five and six p.m. that our excitement was at the highest. While we were at dinner, the commander, Captain Dyer, entered the cabin, and announced, with a look of some anxiety, that the little wind there was having died away, the ship appeared to be fast drifting into the strong current caused by the volcano. We were at this time within a mile of it, and a brig, which was in the offing, actually carried to Malta the report that we were engulphed. The captain, jumping up with a true sailor's exclamation, ordered the boats to be lowered, that her head might be towed round. Everyone rushed on deck to witness the manoeuvre; and as I passed into my own cabin at the moment it was performing, the length of the vessel as it were foreshortening the distance, it appeared as if the next heave must throw us on the fiery island.

I have often wondered that I, who am "coward" enough "*to die a thousand deaths*," under circumstances infinitely less alarming than this really was, did not feel at this moment a sensation of fear, except that it is said the mind cannot receive at the same time two great impressions, and wonder and admiration were then predominant in mine, to the exclusion of every other.

Some officers on boards and my husband of the number, were very desirous to try a landing on the island; but Captain Nesham positively refused a boat for this service, and I think the general feeling was rather a nervous one, when we were near enough to be covered with the showers of black dust or pulverized cinders, and to feel our "good ship" shake to her very keel, from the subterranean thunder that issued from the volcano. But it was awfully magnificent, and long after it had gradually faded from our view, in the shades of night, our ears were on the *qui vive* for the sound of some fresh explosion. Still longer will the remembrance of that sight be vividly impressed on the minds of all who saw it; and though it is now some years since this subterranean wonder appeared, yet it is a subject that can hardly be devoid of interest at any time, to those who love to watch the wonderful works of God, displayed in the extraordinary, as well as daily routine of his great creation.

Whether we consider Graham's Isle as an outbreak from the volcanic vein which has shown itself at intervals in the north of Italy, then southwards at Vesuvius, the Lipari Islands, Etna, and the north of Africa, where the remains of extinct volcanoes are to be seen; or as a sudden burst of fire, which appeared for a time like a meteor on the bosom of the ocean, and almost as suddenly disappeared, leaving no visible trace behind; it certainly may claim a place among the natural phenomena which have at different periods excited our wonder and admiration. Subsequent accounts from Malta mentioned, that the week after the sailing of the *Melville*, a party were sent out by Sir Henry Hotham (who then commanded in the Mediterranean) to make further observations on the volcano.

All appearance of fire and smoke was gone, but a column of water rose to the height of several feet from the crater. They landed on the rock, planted the Union Jack, and named it "Graham's Island," after the first lord of the Admiralty. This was taken down a few days after, by some Neapolitans, who hoisted their own standard, calling it "Sciacca," from the nearest town on the coast of Sicily; but the following week an end was put to the contest, by Neptune claiming it for his own; and a shoal under water, only a few feet below the surface, is all that now remains to mark the site of "Graham's Island."

CHAPTER 8

Gibraltar.—Voyage Home

Through Calpe's straits survey the steepy shore;
Europe and Afric on each other gaze!
Lands of the dark-eyed maid and dusky Moor,
Alike beheld beneath pale Hecate's blaze;
How softly on the Spanish shore she plays.
Disclosing rock, and slope, and forest brown.
Distinct, though darkening with her waning phase;
But Mauritania's giant-shadows frown.
From mountain-cliff to coast descending sombre down.

Childe Harold, Canto 2.

After losing sight of Graham's Island, which formed, as might be supposed, the principal topic of conversation on board the *Melville* for some days after, we continued our course steadily westward, bearing rather too much to the north to see the coast of Africa; and the first land we came in sight of was Cape Gata, the south-eastern promontory of Spain. This is such a proverbially windy point, that there is an old sea song beginning,

Off Cape de Gat,
I lost my hat;

and the master, Mr. W., kept up the charter, on which some one observed, "It must bring us a head wind." The two following days we were coasting along the beautiful shores of Granada; every now and then catching the snowy peaks of the Sierra Nevada, and recalling the descriptions of Washington Irving. In the course of the third night we were off Gibraltar, but as it was blowing very fresh, we lay to for some hours, and, when day dawned, had the advantage of seeing this striking place, for the first time, in a storm of thunder and lightning. It was magnificent to hear the thunder rolling as it were out of the heavy masses of cloud and vapour which covered the top of the rock, with a sound which would have deadened all the artillery even of that mighty fortress; and to see the forked lightning playing down its black and rugged sides.

The thermometer now stood at 68°, twenty degrees lower than when we left Malta, and the rain came down in torrents; but as the day advanced, the storm cleared away, and the sun was shining brilliantly when we anchored before Gibraltar. In a few minutes innumerable boats were putting off from the Ragged Staff with fruit, vegetables, and fresh provisions of every kind (luxuries never more appreciated than after a sea voyage), and those of the *Melville* were soon ready to convey all who wished it on shore.

We were early enough to be in time for the market, which is really one of the sights of the Mediterranean:—every kind of fish, fleshy and fowl; every variety of fruit, flowers, and vegetables; every description of costume, naval and military, civil and religious; almost all the tongues of Europe, and many of Africa, as well as of the East, are here to be met with, and form a most varied and amusing *tableau vivant*; an hour is soon gone in looking at, and listening to, all around you. Some of the gentlemen of our party went to have a canter on the neutral ground, and others to visit the celebrated galleries in the rock; but the heat was so great that I preferred sauntering about the narrow streets, where a shady side may always be found after twelve o'clock, looking into the curious little shops, and seeing the stately Spanish women in their black *mantillas* going to vespers in the different churches.

We dined on shore; saw a sunset (as magnificent as his rising had been) which seemed to tip the chain of hills on the African coast with gold, and went on board again in the cool of the evening. It was a lovely night, and I sat on deck till near eleven, watching the operation of getting "under way." I suppose few things can give a better idea of the advantage of discipline than the working of a large ship; the *Melville's* complement was about seven hundred men, but all moved with such perfect order and quiet, that not a sound was heard on the occasion, but the boatswain's whistle or the word of command from the officer on duty;—it was beautiful!

Looking back, Gibraltar appeared like an illuminated amphitheatre. Above the town, which is built round the bay, villas are dotted quite over the side of the hill, and as all these lighted up for the night, and many of the lights were reflected again into the water, the effect was very striking. Long after the murmur of sounds on the shore had died away, we saw these lights like stars in the distance, till, perfectly wearied out, we were glad to lie down in our comfortable cabins. The next day we had a view of both continents when we went on deck, and saw the white houses of Tangier, and the palm-trees which, grow near the shore, very distinctly; then, bearing up to the north-west, we passed Cape Trafalgar. There was an old quarter-master in the *Melville* who had been in Nelson's ship at the time of the action, and we made him come into our cabin to give us an account of it, and drink to the memory of the hero, Of course one had read it a hundred times before, but it was interesting to have it repeated on the spot by one who had been actually present.

Three of the invalid soldiers died on the passage home; and nowhere does our beautiful burial service sound more solemn and affecting than when, before the ship's company, standing around uncovered, and in the calm of a summer evening, the body is committed to the deep, there to wait until that day when the sea shall be called upon to "*give up her dead.*" When the first and last dreaded separation between soul and body takes place, it matters little in reality what becomes of the latter, whether "*earth be turned to earth*" again, or "*the body to corruption*" in the deep; but still there is something in that heavy sound, that parting of the waters for a second, that ripple on the surface which, for a few moments, marks the grave of a fellow-creature, and then is gone forever, that, once having been seen, can never be forgotten.

We were five days crossing the Bay of Biscay; a dead calm the greater part of the time. Some began to look out impatiently for a breeze, and mutter that "it was no wonder, with women and children on board, we made so little progress;" but this was an exception to the general kindness and attention we experienced, from our kind-hearted old friend, Captain N., to the youngest middy in the gun-room; everything that could be thought of to conduce to our comfort and accommodation was done; our children were petted and played with by the officers, and our favourite dog even was free of the quarter-deck! Life on board ship is so different to what it is on shore, that the novelty alone makes it amusing to a landsman; while the freedom from interruption from without, gives ample time for reading, or the prosecution of any study, provided the weather be as it was during the greater part of our homeward-bound voyage—delightful.

After leaving Trafalgar, however, the monotony of the days was only broken by an occasional ship we hailed, by a flight of Mother Carey's chickens, or by watching the beautiful phosphoric light in the evening from a shoal of passing porpoises; and the wish for land became general. It was therefore with much satisfaction we found ourselves, on the 8th of September, coming up the Channel at the rate of eleven knots an hour, and saw the bonfires on the coast lighted in honour of the coronation of His Majesty William IV. We anchored at Spithead, fired a royal salute (against the stunning effects of which, my Maltese experience of artillery practice had not rendered me proof), and, taking leave of our kind friends on board the *Melville*, once more landed in England.

CHAPTER 9

A Chapter of Less Peaceful "Recollections"

Spain's realms appear, whereon her shepherds tend
Flocks, whose rich fleece right well the vendor knows:
Now must the pastor's arm Ms lambs defend,
For Spain is compassed by unyielding foes;
And all must shield their all,
Or share subjection's woes.—Childe Harold, *Canto 1.*

And now, once more in England, before we again exchange the cold skies of the north for the softer influences of a southern sun, it may not be irrelevant, in these *Recollections of a Rifleman's Wife*, to add a few words connected with the services of that regiment, and some anecdotes which have not before appeared in print; though I should have little hope of communicating the interest with which I have listened to these details, from those who were eyewitnesses or actors in the scenes described, to *my* readers, if it were not my intention to insert some letters from the venerable friend mentioned in the first chapter, the late Chief Justice Day, which are as remarkable for the beauty and perspicuity of the style, as they are for the prophetic spirit in which they were written.

Fortunate were those who, during the course of the long and arduous campaign of the Peninsular war, formed part of the advanced line of the army in Spain. The intuitive sagacity of the Duke, then Lord Wellington, was not the least prominent feature among his rare and distinguished qualities, and he saw at a glance, among those who were immediately brought under his notice, "what stuff" they were made of. Those who joined as volunteers, and who showed themselves active and energetic, were sure to be early recommended for the vacant commissions; and if, instead of idly lounging away in unprofitable indolence the few spare hours which military duties afforded, a young man devoted his time to the study of languages and of the theoretical part of his profession, he qualified himself for those staff situations which were equally honourable and profitable.

The following advice, contained in a letter (enclosing one of introduction to the Duke), might be read with advantage by any young officer; and he to whom it was addressed, and on whom it was not thrown away, has tested, in his long experience of the army, the truth of every word of it.—

I received your letter of the 3rd two or three days ago, just as I was setting off to town, and, agreeable to your wish, enclose you a letter to Lord Wellington, which I sincerely hope may serve you; but of this be sure, that your own conduct will be your best recommendation. You must be not only brave, but active and indefatigable in the discharge of your duty; always forward in courting opportunities of distinguishing yourself, studiously solicitous to acquire a knowledge of your profession, and preserving the highest respect for your superiors, the most unshaken good temper and accommodating disposition among your equals, and a strict discipline, combined with an affectionate feeling for the soldiery. Of all things you must avoid by words or actions to give offence, or to betray a disposition to quarrel. A quarrelsome officer is the greatest nuisance, and ought instantly to be hunted out of the army; for a man of true spirit will reserve the display of his courage for the enemy.

In a large army, many a gallant action is performed, and many instances of individual courage and daring are shown, which never come to the knowledge of a commanding officer; and perhaps there were few regiments in the service where more of these daily occurred than in the Rifle Brigade. In none, perhaps, did a better feeling exist between the officers and men, and which probably contributed much to the uniform success of this gallant corps; for while the strictest military discipline prevailed, kindness and consideration on the one hand, were met by the most respectful, and, in many cases, devoted affection on the other. When not actually engaged with the enemy, and when the weather permitted, the officers were in the habit of joining the men in all kinds of athletic exercises, and the names of Crampton,

Uniacke, and Johnstone will be as well remembered, as the active pro-
moters of cricket, football, rackets, leaping, running, and casting the
stone, as they are for their gallantry in the field.

These amusements, together with hunting and coursing (in which
the subsequently well-known hero of Aliwal took a forward part),
helped to soften "the rugged features of war;" while under their
matchless commander, Sir Andrew Barnard, whose talents as an officer
were equalled by his high and gentleman-like bearing as a man, the
most perfect unanimity and good fellowship prevailed. It was enough
for him to express a wish, where others would issue a command; and,
to the credit of the regiment it may be said, that through the whole
course of the war they never failed in effecting the orders of their
commander, and were never surprised on piquet.

On the 3rd of April, 1811, the Light Division, in consequence of
the ignorance of the guides, were brought unexpectedly in face of
Reynier's rear-guard of 16,000 men before Sabugal. These they re-
pulsed with great gallantry before the third and first divisions could
join in the action, as had been intended by the Duke. In this affair the
43rd particularly distinguished themselves, having taken two guns and
a howitzer, for which the enemy fought hard, literally "*to save their
bacon,*" the gun-carriages being thickly hung with flitches and hams
plundered from the poor Portuguese.

While the Rifles were driving a line of the enemy's skirmishers
before them, through a beautiful chestnut wood, and a private, of the
name of Finn, was taking aim at a Frenchman, a hare started from
under cover of the ferns with which the ground was covered, the
rifle was quickly brought round, and the hare dropped. The officer
to whose company the man belonged, good-naturedly called him to
account for letting the Frenchman escape. "Ah, your honour," said he,
"we can kill a Frenchman any day, but it is not always we can bag a
hare for your supper."

Soon after this, at Fuentes d'Honore, the French had been driven
out of a wood, and were observing rather a more respectful distance
than Riflemen are accustomed to fire at. This man and his comrade
were observed to leave the lines, and walk towards the enemy's out-
post. An officer, who saw them, pointed them out to the serjeant,
suspecting some desertion. "Oh no, sir," was the answer, "it is only for
a little amusement;" and he then watched them go to the banks of the
stream which divided the parties, and after kneeling down to quench
their thirst (for it was a sultry day towards the end of May), took a

deliberate aim, which evidently told on the opposite side; then held up their caps on their rifles to receive the fire in return, and afterwards walk quietly back to their companions.

The coolness of the men in action, and their apparent indifference to anything like danger, I have often heard spoken of by their officers, and it was no wonder, with such materials as then constituted the British Army, that such victories should have been gained against such superior numbers; the feeling seemed to be, that each man had but to do his duty, in perfect confidence that all that skill and forethought, on the part of their leader, could effect, would not be wanting to ensure success.

On the 28th of September the Light Division encamped on the beautiful ground near Scoita. The chestnut-trees here were of a magnificent size. One day a battalion of the Guards were completely sheltered under their widely-spreading branches, during one of the heavy storms of rain which fall in this country in the autumn; and on another occasion a party of six or seven officers, with their servants, found ample accommodation in the hollow trunk of one of them, which made an excellent dining-room.

The general appearance of Portugal is sandy and rocky, but abounding with fine woods; and there are in many parts spots of exquisite beauty, such as Cintra, with its golden groves, the valley of the Mondego, Portalegre, &c. Few had better opportunities than the Light Division (who, in the course of their campaign, traversed the country three times from north to south) of judging of the desolate scene a country presents through which an enemy is retreating ; and the track of the French through Portugal was marked with every species of wanton cruelty and devastation.

The olive-trees, which form the principal wealth of the lower orders of the Portuguese (for, on marrying a daughter, the farmer will give so many of these trees as her dowry), used to be cut down; the wells were poisoned; dead bodies frequently were placed in the closets of the houses in such a way as to fall forward on the doors being opened; the cattle would be ham-strung; and it was no uncommon sight to find the mutilated body of a priest by the roadside, often with his tongue cut out.

After some marching and counter-marching, and again crossing the Aguada, a company of the Rifles were detached to a farm in advance of Attalia, close to Ciudad Rodrigo, by which the supplies of provisions were brought in from Salamanca, and the piquet posted here found it quite expedient to help themselves before forwarding them to headquarters. Sometimes there was enough for both, but it not unfrequently happened that the lion's share left very little for the others. The quarter-master wrote to the officer, requiring all to be sent in; to which the latter returned a very polite answer, couched, by the help of a dictionary, in such abstruse terms as quite puzzled the worthy functionary, who, rather than expose his ignorance by showing the note to the commanding officer, took no further notice of the toll that used to be levied at the farm of Framora.

Deer and wild-boar abounded in the neighbouring woods, and made din agreeable variety in the not overstocked larders of the campaigners. The commissariat had much difficulty in keeping up with the Light Division; and I have often heard the officers say the men were their best purveyors, for hardly were they in action ten minutes before biscuit and brandy, the spoil of some conquered Frenchman, were sure to be brought them.

On the 20th of December the Light Division were reviewed by the duke, on the plain between Guinaldo and Albadon, preparatory to the investment of Ciudad Rodrigo. The weather was tremendous, and the troops used to return at night to their cantonments at Guinaldo with sleet and rain driving in their faces, and frequently obliged to break the ice before they could cross the river. The division, having crossed the Aguada, assembled at the convent of Caridàd, and at nightfall that evening two companies of the 52nd and two of the Rifles carried a fort by a *coup-de-main*, each company attacking a face of the square redoubt. The front ranks jumped into the ditch, and the rear ranks from their shoulders into the works, taking all the garrison prisoners.[1] One officer and a few men only were lost on this occasion; and during the night the fort was converted into a breaching battery, which greatly facilitated the operations of the siege. Of course, I attempt no description of these scenes, but merely endeavour to repeat the conversations of those who were actors in them, assisted by a few rough notes taken at the time; though the many able and interesting accounts of the war which have been published render even this much superfluous.

A few minutes before the engagement began, two young Riflemen were talking together in front of the trenches. "Look there," said one of them to his companion, pointing up to the walls bristling with cannon above their heads, "what would our mothers say" (they were both

1. This is one of the many successful exploits achieved by that distinguished officer, Lord Seaton, of the 52nd.

widows' sons) "if they saw what was preparing for us?"

"Far better they should not," replied his friend; "but what an extravagant fellow you are to have put on that beautiful new *pelisse* for such a night as this."

"Oh!" answered the other, laughing, "I shall be all the better worth taking." Within half an hour their regiment had gained the ramparts by the small breach, and the first speaker was detached with his company to take the enemy in flank, who were opposing the advance of the third division. A mine was sprung, and, amid two or three hundred of the enemy, the gallant General M'Kinnon and this young officer were blown up.

Captain Uniacke was particularly beloved in his own company, and his pay-sergeant, who was afterwards quarter-master in the regiment, was determined he should be buried in consecrated ground. The Spanish priests refused, because he was a heretic; but poor Fairfoot insisted on his being an Irishman, which to them was equivalent with being a Romanist, and permission was given. "I chose out," he afterwards said, in telling the story, "the finest tree in the churchyard of Galleagos, and there I laid his head." Many a soldier who fell that night had nothing to mark his sepulture.

No language can describe the scenes which passed this night in the devoted city, notwithstanding the strenuous efforts of General Picton and Colonel Barnard, aided by the officers, to check the excesses of the soldiery.

> What rein can hold licentious wickedness,
> When down the hill he holds his tierce career?
> We may as bootless spend our vain command
> Upon the enraged soldiers in their spoil,
> As send precepts to the leviathan
> To come ashore.

Dreary was the scene which the next morning's sun rose upon. The blackened and smoking ruins of the still burning town; houses whose inhabitants had either perished or were fled; homeless creatures wandering about, some stupefied, some distracted; broken gun-carriages, scattered arms, and masses of the yet unburied dead; and all this, mixed sometimes with wild shouts and the drunken laughter of the plundering soldier, makes the day after a battle one of the most fearful to look back to.

> The pride, pomp, and circumstance of glorious war

are gone; and death and destruction, in their most appalling forms, alone remain.

At the top of the great breach of Ciudad Rodrigo, thickly strewn with the dead of the "Fighting Third" Division, lay side by side Captain Hardyman and Lieutenant Pearse, of the grenadier company of the 45th. They were two of the handsomest men in the army; were great friends, and universal favourites; and *"in their death they were not divided."*

On returning to their old quarters at Guinaldo, the Light Division were met by the 5th, who were sent to occupy the fallen town. They opened out right and left, presenting arms, and playing the 'British Grenadiers,' in compliment to those who had been more fortunate than themselves in being engaged. Nothing could present a greater contrast than the appearance of the two divisions at this time as seen from a little distance; the soldiers of the former having tied up their uniforms, which they slung to their rifles, while they had dressed themselves out in every variety of costume taken from the plundered city, and which were speedily disposed of at Guinaldo, where a regular fair was established.

Here the troops were allowed time to recover from the fatigue of the siege, and then, turning southward, commenced their march through a hilly and interesting country, containing many towns and villages (leaving the invalids at Castello Branco), to Badajoz, which they reached on the 17th of March, the bands playing 'St. Patrick's day in the morning;' and there are few who are not sensible of the inspiring effect of national music on such an occasion.

The officer who was left in charge of the detachment at Castello Branco, had the good fortune to get one who was obliged to remain on account of health to take his place, and from among the invalids a hundred and twenty-five immediately volunteered to accompany him, and they soon joined the Light Division, who, with the 3rd and 4th, were in the trenches before Badajoz. On the morning of the 20th, an enfilading party opened with twenty guns and eight howitzers, and at nine in the evening Fort Piccarina was stormed and carried by the covering party. During the 21st the Rifles were much employed in the trenches; one party was ordered to fire into the enemy's embrasures, and succeeded in silencing several guns (gabions having been placed in the embrasures).

On the 29th and 30th a breaching battery of eight guns opened on the town, and was nearly silenced by the castle; the next day another battery of twelve, and one of six guns, opened with effect, and the Engineers blew up the dam-head of the Guadiana, on which the town stands,[2] but without letting off the water. On the 5th of April the order was given to storm that night, but it was countermanded, and it was not till the following day that the divisions moved on to the assault. The 3rd Division escaladed the castle, which General Picton succeeded in possessing himself of. The 4th and Light Divisions were severely cut up, and could never have gained the ramparts had not the breaches been turned by the 3rd, who got in at the castle, and the 5th, who escaladed at the Pardeleros Gate, under the command of General Walker, who was severely wounded.

The attack commenced at ten at night, and lasted till two in the morning, during which time the Light and 4th Divisions, though subjected to one of the hottest fires ever sustained, did not cease in their gallant, but ineffectual attacks upon the breaches, defended by *chevaux de frise* of sharpened sword-blades and every other offensive device that Philippon's ingenuity could invent. The loss of the Light Division on this occasion, between killed and wounded, was 976 men, 70 officers, and two volunteers.

For two days and nights Badajoz was a prey to all that the worst passions of men could make it; a sort of pandemonium, from the details of which the mind turns with sickening horror. The wounded were left in the hospital tents till the third day, and were then taken into the town, where they received the greatest kindness from some poor nuns, who, in the general wreck of social life, had been driven out of their convents, and had taken up their temporary abode in a deserted house, devoting themselves to the care of the sick and the dying. Bullock-carts were prepared to convey those who were able to bear it to Elvas, preparatory to embarkation for England; and as the *Recollections* I am very imperfectly depicting are those of one of this party, I must for a time leave the battlefield of Spain, and follow the wounded on their homeward march.

The country from Badajoz to Elvas is, for the most part, flat, but rich and beautifully wooded; the roads were fortunately good, but to every jolt of the spring wagons, the wounded limbs they conveyed were acutely sensitive, and the change, therefore, was most welcome at Abrantes, where boats were provided for their reception. The banks of the Tagus are steeper and much more diversified than those of the Rhine, but, like them, in many parts are covered with vineyards and

2. Or, more properly, the Kivillas, which is a small branch of the Guadiana.

olive-grounds, sloping down to the water's edge. The boats, with their long picturesque lateen sails, as white as snow, were sufficiently commodious; and I have often heard described the luxury of sitting on the gunwale, with a broken leg in the water, eating delicious oranges;— luxury dearly purchased at the expense of much previous suffering. During three days the boats glided down the beautiful stream, and after passing the castle and village of Pinneta, entered the lovely valley of Taneas, the subject of many a pencil.

The strong position of Santarem, long the headquarters of the French army, was on the right bank, and the large towns of Jellada, Salvaterra, and Villa Franca were successively passed, till they reached Alaudra, on the right of the lines of Torres Vedras. At Lisbon the boats were changed, and the little fleet arrived at Belem as the ships in the river were firing a *feu de joie* in honour of the birthday of Ferdinand VII. That of our own king, on the 4th of June, was still more observed; the day was brilliant, there was not a curl on the water, and the report of the salvos of artillery from the ships and forts, the former decked out in all their colours, was very fine. On the 16th the Blue Peter was hoisted, and on the 18th the fleet, consisting of forty-eight sail, and under the convoy of a sloop of war, stood out to sea.

The following letters from Judge Day (the first dated June 13th) show the feeling in England at this time about the operations carrying on in the Peninsula, as well as his own clear views as to the probable result.

I received your letter of the 23rd April with great pleasure and many thanks. It gives a clear and interesting detail of your army, its situation and prospects, and proves that you do not look superficially at the great and awful drama acting before you, but view it as you ought, with a soldier's eye. You have had, indeed, a very long, and to us unaccountable, interval of relaxation and rest. At a time when such heavy drafts have been made from the French army, and so considerable an accession of numbers and strength from the Spaniards to the Allied army, why we should have rested upon our arms through the whole winter and spring, and never interrupted for such a length of time the slumbers and repose of the enemy, I say, to us at a distance from the scene, is unaccountable.

I trust your next will give us the comfort of some active and brilliant operations. The illustrious Wellington will add fresh laurels to his brows before he closes this campaign. I consider him a combination of the two great rival generals of old— of Hannibal and Fabius,—knowing alike when to attack and when to retreat, and alike victorious in both. It is, however, unfortunate for the poor gentleman that he has not some of us wiseacres at his elbow to advise and guide him; some of our sage politicians or feather-bed soldiers, who are very brave over the battle on paper, and know a thousand times better than you blockheads on the spot what course *ought* to be taken.

For instance, had I the command of the army, I should propose instantly to cross the Tonnes (shouting 'Hurrah,' as I passed the glorious plains of Salamanca) and the Douro, and breakfast at Valladolid upon some 8,000 or 10,000 of the Invincibles, make a luncheon of the garrison at Burgos, or mask it, and march on through Vittoria[3] (catching fresh courage from the name), and dine at Bayonne; push on after dinner, before nightfall, for Bordeaux, and take my evening's claret with Barton and Johnson, and the other honest fellows there, at the fountain-head. But I think seriously, if the Spaniards were true to themselves, and seconded, sincerely and ardently, 'the great lord,' as they rightly enough call him, I am sufficiently sanguine to hope he could not only drive the 'grand nation' and their invincible army like sheep out of the Peninsula before him, but would before the end of the campaign erect the standard of insurrection in France.

Meantime, in the north, things are going retrograde. The Allies have lost a great deal of ground, but they have fought with infinite gallantry and skill; retreated with all the regularity of a field-day after every action, without even losing a gun or a pair of colours; killed, it is believed, many more than they have lost, are falling back upon their resources, and drawing the enemy from his; and, I trust, will shortly turn back upon him, and force him to retrace his steps across the Elbe, and even the Rhine.

This, I do not despair, would be the final issue of the campaign, though the Crown Prince and Austria took no part; but the Crown Prince surely cannot prove so steeped in duplicity, so thorough a double dealer, as not to take an active part with us in the rear of the French army, after, all the money he has had from us—after throwing away the scabbard, it would seem, with

---

3. The Battle of Vittoria was gained just one week after this was written.

110

Buonaparte! In that case the latter, placed between two, fires, must retreat precipitately and with infinite disaster. But if Austria joined the cause in which she, as well as the rest of Europe, has so deep an interest; were she to interpose her army from Bohemia, Buonaparte's retreat would become impracticable, and he must capitulate. The latter course of events, perhaps, it would be too much to expect, but I repeat my confident hope, at all events, of a successful issue to the campaign.

Before a year had elapsed, the wounded heroes of Rodrigo and Badajoz were again on their way to rejoin their comrades in the Peninsula.[4] The army were now in their winter quarters, along the line of the Aguada, which was crossed about the middle of May by the whole of the forces, and they continued marching in the highest spirits and the most perfect order after the enemy, who were retiring before them over nearly 200 miles of country, till on the 18th of June they came up with them at St. Milan, and then gave them a foretaste of what they were to receive on a more extended scale at Vittoria. It was here, in consequence of Sir Andrew Barnard's beautiful manoeuvring on the enemy's flank, that a French division was surprised, and one of their brigades made prisoners.

On the morning of the 21st the long-deferred hopes of the army were gratified by seeing the forces of Joseph Buonaparte drawn out in order of battle on the plain, and covering the heights by which the town is protected. Lords Hill and Lynedoch commenced the attack on the flanks of the enemy; and when the Duke's eagle eye perceived that their centre was considerably weakened by the numerous detachments that had been sent to support their wings, he ordered on the 3rd, 4th, and Light Divisions, which carried all before them; and though the French frequently halted and showed fight, giving much

---

4. On passing through the headquarters of the army at Frenéda, one of these officers was invited by the Duke to join the hunt for which he was preparing, and, being well mounted, he gladly availed himself of the honour. The day was beautiful, but the ground very wet. The hounds soon found, and went off at a rapid pace, through an extensive ploughed field, when the Duke, on his celebrated "Copenhagen," and the young Rifleman, whose horse was in good condition (though after a sixteen days' march), were soon separated from the rest of the field. This gave the subaltern an opportunity of admiring the bold riding of his chief, who neither swerved to the right nor left, but took every wall in his way. The fox, followed by three couple of hounds, was often in view, but just as they were looking upon his death as certain, he took to ground, under a rock, from whence the Duke, with his long hunting-whip and a terrier dog, tried ineffectually to dislodge him.

trouble and more fatigue, the pursuit was not abandoned till near eight o'clock that evening.

One hundred and fifty guns were taken, and all their commissariat, luggage, and stores, as well as the pay for the troops, which had not been given out, fell into the hands of the British. Had our cavalry been up, it is supposed the enemy would have been annihilated, so great was the confusion and dismay amongst them towards the end of the day. Lord Lynedoch's movement cut them off from the road to Bayonne; and the one they were obliged to take to Pampeluna, (and before reaching which their last gun was taken,) was most unfavourable for the transport of artillery. I cannot help quoting the following vivid description of this scene from *The Bivouac*.

> The sun was setting, and his last rays fell on a magnificent spectacle: red masses of infantry were seen advancing steadily across the plain, the Horse Artillery at a gallop to the front, to open its fire on the fugitives, the Hussar Brigade charging by the Camino Real, while the 2nd Division, having overcome every obstacle and driven the enemy from its post, was extending over the heights upon the right in line, its arms and appointments flashing gloriously in the fading sunshine of departing day.

The situation of Vittoria is beautiful, on a rising ground, in a fine plain, the River Zadorra describing a graceful curve on the left, and surrounded by a line of hills. The name is said to have been given from having been the scene of some victory in the early history of Spain; it has more than once been the theatre of British prowess, for it was within sight of the town that the Black Prince, at the Battle of Najara, triumphed over the forces of Du Guesclin.

Nothing could be more masterly than the way in which the guns attached to the Light Division were transported across the plain, under the command of Captains Ross and McDonald; the ground being completely intersected with ditches, the officers and gunners would descend into them, and, when the drivers urged on their horses to a gallop, literally putting their shoulders to the wheel, would raise them over with the greatest dexterity. The first gun that was taken that day from the enemy, was by an officer of the Rifles, assisted by two privates and a Portuguese corporal.

While his company were engaged with some cavalry who threatened the right flank, he saw that the French artillery, who were placed on a hill, and enfilading our line, were commencing a retreat, and, calculating on reaching the road before them, he called on the men to follow him, and sprang forward. Five guns passed, but the men, not being in such light marching order, had not been able to keep up with him; in despair he threw himself upon the leading horses of the sixth and checked them: the driver took aim and the shot passed through his cap, but in a moment he dismounted him, and called to the men behind to fire; they did so, one of the horses fell, which effectually stopped the gun, and the rest having by this time come up, the traces were cut, and the three drivers and four gunners were made prisoners. The officer mounted one of the horses, a powerful animal, which, with some difficulty, he prevented from carrying him, *nolens volens*, into the ranks of the enemy, who were posted behind the walls of a churchyard.

There was no time for pitching tents this night, and after the last shots had been fired, the wearied companies lay down in a large furze-brake. Lucky it was for those who did so, that some, from pain, fatigue, and over-excitement, could not sleep, for the furze having been by some accident set on fire, the flames spread with such rapidity, that but for their exertions many lives would have been lost; the armourer-serjeant of the Rifles was so overcome with sleep and wine, that he was only saved by his comrades dragging him by the legs to windward of the burning bushes; and, in running through the thicket, one officer found a soldier of his company counting gold *doubloons* into his wife's lap, quite unconscious of the approaching danger.

The following day the 1st and 3rd battalions of the Rifle Brigade and Ross's guns were sent in pursuit of the fugitives, which they continued till they were under cover of the walls of Pampeluna, having done them as much injury as they could notwithstanding the hindrances thrown in their way by the pouring rain, the broken bridges over swollen streams, and the blazing villages through which they had to follow them.

Out of many instances of individual daring, it is hard to select one, but from its singularity the following may be worth mentioning. As the Rifles were driving a line of skirmishers over a plain, a young lieutenant, of the name of Hamilton, being as usual to the front, was perceived by a French cavalry officer, who rode at him, fancying he would be made an easy prisoner. Instead of waiting, Hamilton ran forward to the rencontre, but the Frenchman, when on the point of closing, wheeled round, putting his horse to a gallop, and was followed by his adversary nearly at the same pace (he was about the fleetest runner in the army), till they reached the edge of a steep cliff, which on that side abruptly terminated the plain. In a moment the Frenchman was off his horse and sliding down the precipice with more haste than dignity; in another moment Hamilton was in the saddle; having gained, not only a horse by this adventure, but having the luck to find the holsters fall of gold; it might have been better for the original possessor had they contained pisto*ls* instead of pisto*les* on this occasion.

The page of history furnishes many instances of battles gained with a great disproportion of numbers. Those of Marathon and Pharsalia in remote times, of Cressy and Agincourt in more modern, will occur to the recollection of every one; but there are few, if any, where the struggle continued for so long, and was attended with such uniform success, as by our army in the Peninsula, from the opening of the campaign at Rolica, in 1808, to the glorious *finale* at Waterloo, in 1815. The French officers who were made prisoners at Vittoria very frankly confessed that their men were completely *démoralisés;* that they had been so long accustomed to defeat, that it was with the greatest difficulty they were made to face the British; and yet I have heard our officers speak in the highest terms of the French bravery as a nation, of their cheerful endurance of hunger and fatigue, and their excellent marching.

The officers of the Light Division, more than any others, had an opportunity of judging of the spirit of *bonhommie* and courtesy for which they are remarkable. Whenever the piquets were sufficiently near, the officers of both armies scarcely ever failed to meet; civilities were interchanged, and often enough a glass of *eau de vie* was drunk to the health of the fair daughters of France and of England. The French on these occasions would frequently regret that, instead of being at war with each other, two such nations should not unite to make common cause against the rest of Europe.

This reminds me of a little circumstance which happened in Portugal, when, after being in pursuit all day, a company of the Rifles came up towards evening with some of the enemy. The captain of the party advanced with a white handkerchief on his sword, and the order was immediately given to cease firing. He said, that, after fighting from daybreak, he and his men would be glad of a little rest, and proposed a truce until morning, to which the English officer readily assented, and invited him and his two subalterns to share their scanty rations of salt-beef, a little cheese, and some rum. The invitation was gladly accepted, and, after dining very sociably together, each party retired to their respective piquets. The next morning came the order to advance, and the pursuit was continued.

About three months after this, one of the English officers, being on piquet on the Dos Casas, close to Fuentes d'Onore, saw an officer, who was lame of one leg, coming towards him from the enemy's lines, who, on a nearer approach, hailed him as an acquaintance. "*Est-ce que vous ne me reconnaissez pas?*" said he, and then proceeded to remind him he had been one of the party at Redinia.

"One of your men," he added, "wounded me the next morning; *mais n'importe, voila la croix de la légion d'honneur.*" He then went on to say that his object in coming down now was not from mere curiosity; that having heard the English were badly off for provisions (which, *par parenthèse,* was true enough), he came to offer him a supply of bread, meat, and wine, which would be brought to a certain place that evening. Of course, no soldier will expose "the poverty of the land," even to a generous foe, so the proposal was declined, with many thanks, and an offer, on the part of the British officer, of different luxuries, which, though he was far from possessing at the moment, he knew the kindness of Colonel Barnard or Baron Alten would enable him to supply had they been accepted.

But to return to the Rifle Brigade, who, after much marching and countermarching in the passes and over the mountains of the Pyrenees, were allowed a fortnight's rest at the pretty town of St. Estevan, in a beautiful valley of the same name. During the halt here, the rain came down in such torrents as are only seen in mountainous districts; but the kindness and hospitality of the inhabitants more than made up for so unfavourable a specimen of the weather. In breaking up from their comfortable cantonments, they next advanced towards the Bidassao, On the march, the Duke told Sir Andrew Barnard that if they could move on two or three miles farther, they would fall in with the French at the bridge of Zanci.

The overpowering heat of the day (28th of July) and the unusual length of the march obliged the rest of the army to halt; but the battalion answered their leader's appeal, and, moving on, soon broke across the bridge, separating one French brigade from another; the one in the rear were made prisoners; and such was the enthusiasm of the men, that even those who (from being footsore) were left under charge of an officer in the rear, advanced so rapidly, that descending the wood they crossed the river and attacked the French column behind, at the same time that the leading company were "*amusing*" them in front! All the baggage fell into the hands of the Light Division, and some useful maps and books were not the least valuable part of the spoil. After a wild bivouac that night, they moved forward next day to the plains before Vera, where they remained for some time, and were able, not only to recruit themselves, but to attend to the poor horses, who were by this time lamentably out of condition; many of them suffering from galled backs, &c.

News from the "far west" cheered our army while here; the last despatches from England bringing the account of the capture of the Chesapeake by the Shannon, under the gallant Brooke. The following extract, from the letters before quoted, will give an idea of what was going on in other parts of the Continent at this period:—

I have received, with the greatest satisfaction and delight, your three letters giving an account of the brilliant victories of San Milan, Vittoria, and the Pyrenees. They were the most interesting details I have anywhere seen of victories which have elevated the fame of the British army beyond any other in the world, and have advanced your commander even be- yond his own glory. We are going to erect a splendid monument to him in this city (Dublin); above £10,000 is already subscribed among us. But really it is to be lamented, and if I might venture to criticize any part of his conduct, I should say it was very reprehensible, that he should expose his person in the way he does in every action, for in his life the fate of Europe and of the civilized world is deeply involved.

Sir John Hope succeeds the noble Graham in command, and is a brave and intelligent officer. You give me credit for my powers of vaticination, and certainly, as far as you have gone, you must allow my prophecy has been correct; but I doubt whether I must not balance between two lines for your future operations,—whether I shall send you to sup, as I intended, with our friends at Bordeaux, where you would be sure of what we Paddies like, a bottle of good claret and a cordial welcome, or whether Toulon would not be still more eligible. The former line would carry you along the coast, where you would be attended by transports, and so on to La Vendée, where you would be received with rapture, and might head a formidable insurrection; the latter would conduct you to the fleet.

That one or the other of these objects will be accomplished,

I venture to stake my prophetic credit upon. The successes in Germany are most exhilarating. The tyrant seems almost hemmed in, and his personal escape very doubtful; the Crown Prince pressing upon Dresden to the northward, Blücher reinforced by Bensingen's 80,000 to the eastward, the Austrian grand army to the southward, and no way for him to get off save to the westward, by Frankfort, or some of the towns on the Rhine, and this cannot be accomplished for his army, unless by what I think is very unlikely, a sanguinary and decisive victory. In Italy, too, the successes are considerable, and the prospects flattering. All this promises at least a speedy peace upon the terms of Buonaparte falling within the Rhine, the Alps, and the Pyrenees, or possibly a revolution, and the extinction of this scourge of the human race.

After driving the French columns through the different passes of the Pyrenees, the Duke determined on dispossessing them from the tops of the mountains, many of which they occupied in force; and it fell to the lot of the 1st and 3rd battalions of the Rifle Brigade to dislodge them from a high conical hill covered with tall ferns, at that time dripping with wet, so that the men and officers, in climbing up the long ascent (so steep in some places that they were obliged to use their hands), were thoroughly drenched from head to foot. However, the skirmishers kept a good line, having companies in close order supporting, and succeeded in reaching the *plateau* on the summit, occupied by the enemy, who at the same time were charged by the skirmishers of the 1st and 3rd battalions, who made their way up on the other side.

The French fire was incessant; but the casualties were comparatively few, as the shots only told on the heads or on the knees of the assailants, from their peculiar position while climbing the long ascent. Scarcely was the hill gained,—known ever afterwards as "Colonel Barnard's Hill,"—than they witnessed a brilliant charge, executed by the 36th regiment, on an opposite eminence, from which they were equally successful in expelling the French.

Having now returned to their old encampment between the Bidassao and Lasacca, some of the officers obtained leave of absence for a few days, in order to witness the storming of St. Sebastian. The country along the banks of the river is mountainous and very picturesque, and before reaching the fortress the view opened on widely spreading orchards, the trees of which were bending under the weight of the most tempting-looking fruit. On arriving, they found the army ready for the assault, which took place at eleven a.m., on the 31st of August, under a brilliant sun. The fighting on both sides was tremendous, and it would have been impossible for the troops to get in but for the singularly well-directed fire of our artillery from the surrounding hills and batteries.

The shots appeared to strike but a few yards over the heads of the advancing columns, slaughtering the enemy, and destroying their defences along the ramparts; and, notwithstanding their gallantry and skill, the town was carried, and, soon after, the castle. The young officer whom I mentioned before as having taken the Frenchman's horse, was shot through the head and in two or three parts of the body, and was brought from the top of the breach by a friend, apparently in a hopeless state, from the severe nature of his wounds; but he was living a few years since (and may be still) in the north of Ireland.

It was here that Sir Richard Fletcher, who commanded the Engineers, received his death wound, while directing a battery of sixty-four pounders, brought from the frigate which co-operated in the siege. The shot went through his head, and he fell without a groan, universally regretted by the army, as well as by his own branch of the profession; for to great military skill and bravery he united the most pleasing and gentleman-like bearing.

On returning to the camp the following night, in a tremendous storm, the amateur spectators of the fall of St. Sebastian were indebted to the sagacity of their horses for their safe arrival there, for, besides being quite ignorant of the road, the perfect darkness of the night was only broken by vivid flashes of lightning, which served to show them the dangerous paths (frequently at the very verge of a precipice) which the surefooted animals were treading. During this storm, the French, who were coming to the support of St. Sebastian, hearing of the fall of the place, endeavoured to regain their own side of the Bidassao, by forcing the piquets of the 2nd Rifles, at the bridge. With overpowering numbers they effected their retreat, but not without severe loss; for besides those that were killed, many were drowned in the torrent. The two companies of the Rifles each lost their captain.

On the 7th of October the army was in motion, and the Light Division were ordered to open the way into France, through the pass of Vera. The affair commenced by the 3rd battalion of the Rifles taking a sugar-loaf hill which stood forward as if to defend the little town and entrance. The eyes of the whole division were upon this little band, and almost every officer could be distinguished leading on his men, and, under the command of Colonel Boss, rarely has a thing been done in neater style: though exposed to a severe fire, the Riflemen never returned a shot until within a few yards of the summit, and then, *one* rush was sufficient to enable them to crown it. The mouth of the pass being thus opened, the two brigades advanced; one to the left, the other to the right, of the winding and narrow road. In the attack on a star fort, the 2nd battalion suffered severely, losing six of their officers, but, with the assistance of the 52nd, who much distinguished themselves on the occasion, they bore down all opposition.

The 1st battalion was even more fortunate on the right, for Colonel Barnard, by his flanking movement, drove the enemy from the strong position they had successively occupied, with little loss to his brigade; and that evening afforded the long and ardently desired view into the rich plains of France, covered with towns and villages, interspersed with villas and vineyards, and clothed with flocks and herds. This fair land was soon to be made the theatre of war; but, owing to the timely and judicious orders of the Duke of Wellington, and the superior discipline of *his* army, was free from those sufferings to which its soldiers, on a similar occasion, had subjected unhappy Portugal.

Before entering another country, it is only justice to that we are leaving to record, though with a feeble pen, some of the sentiments I have often heard expressed by those whose long experience in it, under the most trying circumstances of war, gave them an opportunity of judging of the character of a people, whose sons they found honourable, generous, and hospitable, and whose daughters were alike virtuous and interesting.

With the higher ranks of society, or with the inhabitants of towns, they came little in contact; the duty of the Light Division generally placed them in the wild parts of the country, on the tops of mountains, in the passes, and watching the fords of rivers. The features of this noble country are strongly marked: lofty *sierras* divide nearly all the provinces; vast plains are succeeded by extensive woods; and the scenery of some of the rivers, particularly that of the Ebro, approaches almost to the sublime. I believe there are few who went through the campaign in Spain, who would not gladly return to visit, under happier circumstances, those from whom they received so much genuine and unaffected kindness.

The breaking up of the weather having rendered the roads impracticable for artillery, the Rifles were sent to occupy La Rhune, the highest peak of the Lower Pyrenees, where they remained until the end of November. Inured as they were to hardships, their sufferings here exceeded what they had previously gone through. The rain fell in torrents, except when congealed by the cold into heavy masses of driving snow, and it was with the greatest difficulty they procured sufficient fuel to cook their scanty rations. Such was the severity of the weather, that, though the sentries were each allowed a blanket to wear over his great coat, few nights passed in which one would not be found frozen to death on his post; and one night in particular, several horses perished from the intensity of the cold. Meanwhile, the French, under Soult, were constructing two lines of forts and breastworks, to impede the entrance of our troops, availing themselves of the advanced hill called Petite La Rhune, the natural strength of which they increased with their usual skill.

On the morning of the 9th the welcome order was issued to advance the following day; and as they descended that horrible hill, I believe it was the determination of every man and officer rather to die on the plain than return to it, though Petite La Rhone, bristling with the enemy's bayonets behind its rocks and walls, presented a formidable front to their approach. Long before day the regiments of the division took up their several posts, without any noise, close upon the enemy's lines; and when it was sufficiently light to see their way, each advanced as ordered. The Rifles commenced by turning and attacking the right; the 43rd took them in front, and the 52nd on the left; and so rapidly and effectually had "every man done his duty," that in the course of a few minutes the three British regiments met amidst the French tents, which they had not even time to strike!

The 43rd suffered severely on this occasion, and lost some promising officers; and to the Rifles the victory was not without its alloy, for it deprived them for a time of the presence of their beloved commander. Sir Andrew Barnard, who, while changing the position of the brigade, to oblige a battery of the enemy, to whose fire they were exposed, to alter their range, received a ball through the chest, which lodged in the shoulder-bone; however, by the blessing of God, his recovery (aided by his own unruffled temper) was so complete, that he was ready again to lead them on at the battle of Toulouse. When the regiments re-formed, the division advanced in parallel lines, with the other columns, to the general attack, and in the course of the day succeeded in forcing those formidable works, which had cost Soult, his army, and the peasants of the country, so much time and trouble to construct. This day the army crossed the Nivelle.

The Château d'Arcangues (which they made as strong as possible) was the next post occupied by the Rifles, and the 52nd and 43rd took up their quarters in a small church and village on the left. This advanced part of the line was the scene of daily skirmishes. On the 9th of December a cloud of French light troops occupied the brow of a hill, separated from the *château* by a very narrow valley, and, ensconcing themselves in a number of small houses, and concealed by the inequality of the ground, maintained a sharp tirillade, which lasted from morning till night.

The Rifles fought to disadvantage, as their position was overlooked, and they could not in turn attack the enemy, who were supported by columns posted to their rear, on a plateau which stretched towards Bayonne; however, a sub-division, who occupied a small orchard, kept up a fire from behind the trees, and towards evening there was scarcely one which did not contain some of the enemy's well-directed balls; during this day the incessant roll of musketry on the left told that the 43rd and 52nd were not idle. From the difficulty of recruiting at home, six Spaniards were now added to every company, and oh this and other occasions they evinced great spirit and steadiness, proving that had they been well officered, they would have made excellent and efficient soldiers.

On the 13th of this month Lord Hill gained a brilliant victory over Soult, who attacked him with nearly his whole army, though, owing to the impassable state of the Neive, from the recent heavy rains, his lordship was almost unsupported: it is a singular fact that about 1,500 French in this engagement lay *bayoneted* under the walls of that very town where the weapon was first invented. The victory under the walls of Bayonne terminated the brilliant campaign of 1813,—a campaign planned with combination and judgment, and executed with energy and skill.

When we consider the state of Europe at the time our small army first entered the Mondego, in 1808; when we remember that Portugal was humbled to the dust, that the warlike spirit of Spain was extinguished, and that the lethargy of her government afforded no assistance to those who were combating in her cause; that the supplies from home were always scant and slow in arriving; may we not, with the deepest reverence and the most heartfelt gratitude, believe that "the God of battles" blessed our arms, and that, under his Almighty will, the illustrious Wellington was the instrument for redressing the wrongs of nations and restoring peace to Europe?

The events of 1814 and 15, up to the glorious *finale* of Waterloo, require far more able delineation and a more extended space than the writer or her little book are capable of giving, and this brief and imperfect sketch will therefore conclude with one more quotation from the letters of Judge Day, dated December 10th, 1818.

> I long to hear of the full completion of my prophecy, and of his lordship's quaffing Côte Rôtie at the fountain-head. Further than Bordeaux, my notion is, you will have no occasion to proceed: the Corsican's career is at an end, the Battle of Leipsic sealed his fate; and, still inspired by my prophetic spirit, I pronounce, without hesitation, that we shall soon see the Bourbons reinstated on the throne of their ancestors, a counter-revolution throughout Europe, and the old order of things fully restored. The Allies have already crossed the Rhine, on their way into France, signifying they will not treat for peace with Buonaparte; the Texel and Scheldt fleets are upon the point of declaring against him; all his veterans have perished or are prisoners; his raw conscripts, *you* know, will not fight;—then what is there to impede the march of the 300,000 Allies to Paris? Nothing but what I predict, a general insurrection through France in favour of the old family.

June 1815 saw the fulfilment of this prediction, and Louis XVIII. reinstated, though but for a time, on the throne of his ancestors.

www.ingramcontent.com/pod-product-compliance
Lightning Source LLC
Chambersburg PA
CBHW031900090426
42741CB00005B/578